The Pocket
Small B
Owner'
Taxes

Brian Germer

ALLWORTH PRESS
NEW YORK

This book is dedicated to my wife and best friend, my two children, and my family for all the love and support.

This book is designed to provide accurate and authoritative information with respect to the subject matter covered. It is sold with the understanding that the publisher is not engaged in rendering legal, accounting, or other professional services. If legal advice or other expert assistance is required, the services of a competent attorney, accountant, or other professional person should be sought. While every attempt is made to provide accurate information, the author and publisher cannot be held accountable for any errors or omissions.

Allworth Press books may be purchased in bulk at special discounts for sales promotion, corporate gifts, fund-raising, or educational purposes. Special editions can also be created to specifications. For details, contact the Special Sales Department, Allworth Press, 307 West 36th Street, 11th Floor, New York, NY 10018 or info@skyhorsepublishing.com.

15 14 13 12 11   5 4 3 2 1

Published by Allworth Press
An imprint of Skyhorse Publishing, Inc.
307 West 36th Street, 11th Floor, New York, NY 10018.

Allworth Press® is a registered trademark of Skyhorse Publishing, Inc.®, a Delaware corporation.

www.allworth.com

Cover design by Brian Peterson

Library of Congress Cataloging-in-Publication Data

Germer, Brian.
    The pocket small business owner's guide to taxes / by Brian Germer.
      p. cm.
    Includes index.
    ISBN 978-1-58115-920-2 (pbk. : alk. paper)
    1. Small business–Taxation–United States. 2. Small business–United States–Accounting.
    I. Title.
      HD2346.U5G47 2012
      343.7306'8–dc23
                        2012022755

Printed in the United States of America

Table of Contents

Introduction

"Over and over again courts have said there is nothing sinister in so arranging one's affairs as to keep taxes as low as possible. Everyone does so, rich or poor; and all do right, for nobody owes any public duty to pay more than the law demands . . ."

—Judge Learned Hand

The above quote perfectly encapsulates the most effective way for small business owners to maximize deductions and keep taxes as low as possible, and that is done by first finding what the law demands and then arranging one's affairs to meet what the law requires. Too many small businesses owners do not take the time to dig in and learn tax deduction rules, and so they end up failing to take advantage of important deductions they are permitted to take, while taking other deductions they are not even entitled to. Even worse, many small business owners keep very poor records to document the deductions they do claim, which is a recipe for disaster if they are ever audited.

On the other hand, small business owners should not spend too much time learning every single exception and nuance of the tax code. One of the biggest problems in the digital age is that there is too much information available out there, and some do-it-yourself business owners take the concept way too far and waste time that could be better spent on more important aspects of their business. You only have a finite amount of time to manage your business, so you should only concentrate on the essential tax fundamentals and rules that small business owners need to understand and leave the rest to your tax professional.

This book is designed to provide the small business owners with a practical and balanced understanding of what the law demands. The practical nature of the information comes from the fact that I have been working over twelve years in the trenches with small business owners as a CPA in public accounting firms, and much of the information and advice comes straight from that experience, as well as the experience of my mentors, who have been in the business for over thirty years. The information is balanced in that it provides only what you need to know as a small business owner. Tax rules are extremely complex and always changing, but you do not need to know everything in order to maximize your deductions and keep solid documentation. This book provides you with the essentials so that you can work more effectively with your tax professional at maximizing your deductions and avoiding problems with the IRS.

This book is designed for new and veteran small business owners alike who are active owners of their businesses. Whether you have a single-owner business, a family-owned business, or are one of many owners of a larger business, you are sure to find useful information that will help you maximize your deductions. However, if you are primarily a passive investor or a limited owner who is not actively involved in a business, this book may not be what you are looking for.

The structure of the book is divided into three parts:

- Part I covers the tax and accounting essentials that you should understand as a small business owner, which are the basic fundamentals that serve as the foundation for the rest of the book.

- Part II provides an overview for those choosing a business structure or reconsidering their existing business entity. It also provides invaluable information on crucial S corporation and LLC tax issues.

- Finally, Part III gets to the tax rules that will enable you to maximize deductions for your business. It is not meant to be a complete, exhaustive study of all the tax deductions and strategies, but concentrated study of the most popular deductions.

PART I
Essentials for the Small Business Owner

Chapter 1

SMALL BUSINESS
TAXATION BASICS

I t has been over twenty-five years since the last major overhaul of the federal tax code (the Tax Reform Act of 1986), and more than 15,000 changes have been made since then, many of which were made in the last decade. Ever since the initial "Bush Tax Cuts" of 2001, each year brought on newly phased-in changes and extended tax benefits. In 2010, many thought all the expiring tax provisions would return the tax code to its pre-2001 condition, but then the politicians sent us into double overtime by extending a majority of the 2010 rules for two more years, and now we are in limbo with what I like to call the "Temporary Tax Code."

We can only assume that big changes and tax increases are on the horizon; however, not knowing exactly what that will look like makes long-term tax planning very difficult. This uncertainty has likely created some apathy among small business owners attempting to understand the current tax rules. After all, why learn rules that will soon be replaced with new rules? Well, while I would not recommend a detailed analysis of the current tax code, it is important to understand the basic principles underlying the current tax code—especially those that will likely remain in effect even after major reform.

This brief chapter will provide an overview of the tax basics that every small business owner should understand. In addition to explaining the difference between the self-employed and employee shareholders, the chapter walks through the major categories of taxes that your business will likely face.

Are You Self-Employed or an Employee?

Most small business owners have a bit of an identity crisis when it comes to understanding how they are classified for tax purposes, as most assume they are self-employed if they are an owner of a business. To add to the confusion, mortgage underwriters and banks have their own rules on what makes someone self-employed, so this identity crisis is understandable. Unfortunately, the distinction between employee and self-employed is critically important when learning about small business taxation, so you will need to set aside any pre-conceived notions of who you are for tax purposes before proceeding any further in this book.

If you are a sole proprietor, a partner in a partnership, a member in a limited liability company, or an owner of any other type of entity taxed as a partnership, you are self-employed. You do not receive wages and instead take draws on your share of distributive income from the business. If you are a shareholder in a C or S corporation, you are an employee. Even though there are special rules for more than 2 percent shareholders of S corporations and more than 10 percent shareholders of C corporations, they are still employees for the purpose of most tax rules. As you read through this book, it is important you remember how you are classified as there are many references throughout the book to self-employed owners and shareholders employees.

Self-Employment Tax and the Corporate Equivalent

For most small business owners your main tax frustration is likely the self-employment tax, or the corporate equivalent of the tax if you are a shareholder employee. The first profitable year as a small business owner is usually a shocker, and you quickly realize the dramatic impact that the self-employment tax has on your tax liability. In fact, the tax is likely one of the main reasons that you are reading this book, as you are likely looking for any methods available to minimize this tax levied on business owners, which can seem outright unfair at times when you compare it to the taxes paid by non-owner employees.

If you are a new small business owner, or you have never had a tax professional explain the self-employment tax to you, it is basically a combination of the employee and employer portions of Social Security and Medicare tax, which are discussed in more detail in chapter 6. Part of the joy of owning a business is that the IRS sees you as both employee and employer, so you get to pay double the Social Security and Medicare tax, but if it is any consolation, Uncle Sam lets you deduct the employer portion. Self-employed business owners generally pay self-employment tax on their distributive share of income, while shareholder employees pay the corporate equivalent of self-employment tax on their wages. Strategies on minimizing this tax by using an LLC or S corporation are discussed in Part II of this book.

Income Tax

Regardless of how your entity is structured, some form of income or loss from your business is reported on or flows to your individual tax return, so the individual income tax will always be a part of your overall tax on income from your business. In fact, make sure your tax professional goes over your individual tax returns with you each year so that you have a good idea of what your tax bracket is and what each additional dollar of deduction saves you in taxes. Below is a table with the taxable income ranges for the current tax brackets in case you are not sure of your current marginal tax rate.

2012 Individual Income Tax Brackets				
Tax Bracket	Taxable Income Ranges By Filing Status			
	Single		Married Filing Joint	
10%	$ - to $ 8,700		$ - to $ 17,400	
15%	8,700	35,350	17,400	70,700
25%	35,350	85,650	70,700	142,700
28%	85,650	178,650	142,700	217,450
33%	178,650	388,350	217,450	388,350
35%	388,350	. . . .	388,350	. . . .

Currently, income tax rates are at all time lows, but that is only likely to last through the end of 2012, when the current rates are set to expire and return to something resembling the pre-2001 tax rates. The politicians may intervene, but most small business owners should just plan on a tax increase of around 3 percent in 2013 to be on the safe side for budgeting purposes.

PAYROLL TAXES

If you hire employees, you not only have to pay employer Social Security and Medicare tax on their wages, but also federal and state unemployment tax, and any other state payroll taxes. In addition to the cost, there is a lot of complexity involved as payroll has to be processed regularly, tax deposits have to be paid, and quarterly and annual returns have to be filed. If you have employees, or are thinking about hiring employees or subcontracted labor, you will need to read chapter 6, as it can help you avoid some very costly mistakes.

PENALTIES, FEES, AND OTHER NEW REVENUE RAISERS

No politician wants to be the one who voted for increasing or creating new taxes, but they also want to appear fiscally responsible when passing new spending bills, so they are often faced with the dilemma of how to raise revenue without raising taxes. Well, leave it to the clever career politicians in Washington to find a way to have their cake and eat it too, as they have created several new revenue raisers structured as penalties and fees that affect small business owners. Chief among them are the late-filing penalties for owners of S corporations and entities taxed as a partnership for tax purposes. In chapters 9 and 10, I provide important information on how to request abatement of these penalties, which seem to be increasing each year.

The trend of raising revenue through penalties and fees assessed on small business is a very disturbing trend, and it has never been more important for small business owners to educate themselves on tax rules and engage a quality tax professional who can help them avoid these disguised taxes.

STATE AND LOCAL TAXES

In addition to the clever politicians in Washington, states have had to get very clever with taxes and fees to survive in this recessionary economy. Income, sales & use, excise, franchise, and property taxes have all been increased or more strictly enforced. Many states have even resorted to minimum taxes on small businesses, and sometimes certain business structures are taxed much more heavily than other types of entities simply because of how the laws are written, which I discuss more in chapter 8. If that isn't enough, even local governments have increased business taxes, fees, and licenses.

With all these different levels of taxation, it is important that you stay informed on state and local rules or engage a professional who specializes in these rules. Simple mistakes can be very costly, and states are doing all they can to collect unreported taxes and fees.

Chapter 2

BUSINESS INCOME: WHERE IT ALL BEGINS

When meeting with new clients who are starting a business, I often hear the same problem—they are earning too much money from their side project that has grown into a full-time operation and they want to know how to minimize their tax liability. This is a great problem to have, and hopefully this is where it all started for you as well, as it is definitely the easier path to starting a business.

Don't get me wrong—I am not saying that businesses that start out with start-up costs and little to no income cannot succeed. In fact, I have witnessed first-hand some great success stories where hard-working entrepreneurs dug in and built some strong, profitable companies that allowed them to recover their initial investments. However, for every one of these success stories, I can quickly think of four or more failures where entities were formed, start-up costs were incurred, and the businesses went on and on without really ever creating a significant stream of income.

Whether or not your business is generating income yet, it is important to understand what taxable business income is and what it is not. Granted, it is not as exciting as business deductions; however, there are many types of income that business owners overlook or do not consider, so an overview should definitely be beneficial.

WHAT IS TAXABLE BUSINESS INCOME?

Maybe it would have been better to start with what the IRS does not consider taxable income since Internal Revenue Code §61 answers this question broadly by including "all income from whatever source, except for those items specifically excluded by the Code." Basically, George Harrison had it right and we should be glad they do not take it all.

A majority of the receipts received by your business—whether sales of product or service—are going to fall under this all-encompassing category of "all income from whatever source", but there are sources of taxable income that many small business owners do not consider.

Bartered or Traded Goods or Services

Occasionally, transactions between businesses involve non-traditional forms of payment. For example, a company may receive equipment in exchange for its services, or it may trade services with another business. According to Treasury Regulation 1.61-2(d), the fair market value of the goods or services received in the exchange must be included in income. If it is an exchange of services, the mutually agreed upon fair market value will be accepted as the fair market value unless that value can be show to be otherwise.

Recoveries

Businesses can receive a number of recoveries of items previously deducted during a typically taxable year, and even

Bartered Goods and Services Example

A self-employed locksmith saves the day for a computer products company after an intern broke a key in the door. While re-keying the doors, the locksmith starts talking with a salesman about the latest tablets they have on sale, and he decides he needs one for his business. The owner of the computer products company agrees to give him one in exchange for his locksmith services. The locksmith must record income equal to the fair market value of the tablet; however, since it will be used in his business, he also gets to record it as a fixed asset and deduct depreciation on the tablet.

though they are often offset against the related expense, they are essentially income—especially if there is not a current related expense to offset against. The most common recoveries include: insurance refunds, collections of bad debt previously written off, rebates, and vendor refunds. Most of the time, recoveries are fairly immaterial in amount, but any material amounts should probably be classified as "other income" on your tax return so that they can be easily traced in the event of an audit.

Recovery Income Example

ABC HVAC Company pays workers compensation insurance each month and then each year they are audited. After the most recent audit, their insurance company determined that ABC was due a refund of $800. If ABC has more than $800 in current year workers compensation expense, the recovery can simply be offset against the expense. Instead of reporting it as income on the tax return, the expense is simply reduced by the refund.

Cancellation of Debt

Unfortunately, cancellation of debt income has become far too common due to the recession. To make matters worse, it is often a complex and circumstantial tax matter that you will need to discuss with your tax professional. Nevertheless, as a business owner you need to be aware of the fact that you could have taxable income from debt that is cancelled or forgiven by a creditor unless your business is bankrupt, insolvent (your liabilities exceed your assets), or a farming operation and the debt was qualified farm indebtedness. Also, if the cancelled debt is qualified as real property business debt, then the cancellation does not necessarily create income, but instead it reduces your tax benefits or your basis in the asset.

If you are in foreclosure on a business property or you are negotiating with credit card companies due to financial difficulties, please contact your tax professional as soon as possible. They will be able to determine if you will have taxable income as a result of the debt cancellation and put together some tax planning well before you receive the 1099-C, which is the IRS form that your creditor will use to report the amount of cancelled debt to the IRS.

Example

NW Renovation, Inc., a successful remodeling business during the housing boom, starting flipping homes and making considerable profits until the housing market crash left them upside down on several homes still in their inventory. The company became insolvent, the homes went into foreclosure, and $150,000 in mortgage debt was cancelled. While the $150,000 in cancelled debt would not be income due to the insolvency, it would reduce NW Renovation's tax benefit carryforwards (net operating losses, credits, and capital losses) or the basis in its assets.

What Is Not Taxable Income?

Now to the items explicitly excluded from income by the IRS. Many of these exclusions are straightforward, but they are worth noting as there are always questions stemming from these non-taxable sources.

- **Gifts.** Regardless of the amount received, gifts and inheritances are never subject to income tax. This is a common question raised in family businesses even though it really only becomes an issue for the giver of the gift.

- **Return of capital.** Generally, if you get back what you invested into a business, then it is not taxable.

- **Loan repayments.** If the business repays a bona fide loan, the repayment of principal is not income.

- **Life insurance proceeds.** Generally, life insurance proceeds received by a business are not taxable income, which makes sense given that premiums are non-deductible.

When Does It Become Taxable Income?

Once you have a good understanding of what taxable income is, the more important question of when it is reported as income arises. Most small business owners do not ask this question until it is nearing the end of the year, but it is an important concept to understand at all times during the taxable year.

- **Cash Basis**—If your business reports on the cash basis of accounting, income is reported when payment is received. Even though you have completed the work and sent an invoice, the income is not reported to the IRS until you actually receive the customer's payment.

- **Accrual Basis**—If your business does not qualify for cash basis, or it was purposely set up on the accrual basis of accounting, then income is reported when it is earned. Generally, this would be the point at which you invoice a customer and all the events have occurred that were required to earn the income.

These accounting methods are explained in more detail in chapter 7.

SERVICE BUSINESS INCOME REPORTING ISSUES

If the primary business activity of your business is providing services to customers or clients, and your business is a non-incorporated entity (LLC, LLP, partnership or sole proprietorship), then your business should receive Form 1099-MISC from your customers or clients from whom you received $600 or more in a taxable year. However, this does not mean that you only have to report income over the filing threshold of $600, or that you only have to report income equal to the totals from the 1099-MISC forms you receive. You are taxed on all business income regardless of whether or not you receive a 1099-MISC. In fact, one of the main audit techniques used by the IRS is to go through all the bank statements and reconcile the deposits to your reported income, so it is essential that all business income be reported.

Chapter 3

Cost of Goods Sold: Tracking the Flow of Costs

If you provide services, you can bypass this section and proceed straight to deductions; however, if your business makes or buys goods to sell, this section contains foundational information that will help you correctly track the flow of costs within your organization for accounting and tax purposes.

What Is Cost of Goods Sold?

If you are a manufacturer, wholesaler, retailer, or any other business that makes, buys, or sells goods to produce income, you have to account for many more costs than a service business in order to correctly calculate your net income. For accounting purposes, you have to match revenue from the sale of goods to the costs associated with the goods that were sold, as the costs associated with inventory that is still on hand would not be deducted until later sold. The costs, which are associated with the goods that were sold, make up cost of goods sold, which is deducted from gross receipts to arrive at gross income (or gross profit). In order to calculate cost of goods sold, inventory values have to be calculated at the beginning and end of the year, and procedures have to be set up to carefully track the flow of costs related to the goods to be sold.

When Is Inventory Required?

For tax purposes, the IRS requires inventories when their use is necessary in order to clearly reflect income. For businesses that make or buy goods to sell, the requirement to report inventory is obvious as income could not be calculated accurately without it; however, when it comes to service businesses that also sell goods, the requirement is not always that clear. Materials and supplies that are an integral part of the services provided by a business are not necessarily inventory. These incidental materials or supplies may be expensed as long as the result is a clear reflection of income. However, if the materials and supplies were an income-producing

---

Example

A locksmith business primarily provides services, whether it is helping people with emergency car lockouts or re-keying doors, but they also sell a large amount of keys, locks, and other security equipment that can make up a large portion of their gross receipts. Many locksmiths also keep a material amount of these items on hand so that they are ready for any call. If expensing these items does not result in a clear reflection of income, then the business would be required to determine beginning and year-end inventory and calculate cost of goods sold.

Example

A medical office provides a service, and even though they may use materials and supplies in the course of providing their services, the materials and supplies used would not be inventory. However, if a naturopathic clinic sold supplements in addition to their services, and the supplements were billed separately, then the clinic may need to report an inventory—especially if the supplements are a material source of revenue for the clinic. In a case like this, you should definitely consult with your tax professional to determine the best approach based on your circumstances as there are a number of recent court cases that support not reporting inventory for smaller service businesses.

---

factor for the service business, then most of the time an inventory would be required.

How Do I Calculate Cost of Goods Sold?

To determine the deductible costs associated with goods sold in a particular tax year or reporting period, you will need to have a value for the inventory at both the beginning and end of the year or reporting period. For a tax year-end reporting, this value should be based on an actual physical count, but interim financial statements can be based on a calculation from your inventory software. Generally, the inventory should be valued at cost or the lower of cost or market value. For manufacturers, the inventory balance would include:

- The total cost of raw materials,
- work in process,
- finished goods, and
- materials and supplies used in manufacturing the goods.

The Basic Cost of Goods Sold Formula

Once you have beginning and ending inventory values, the following basic formula would be used to calculate cost of goods sold:

Beginning Inventory + Purchases − Ending Inventory = Cost of Goods Sold

---

For a manufacturing business, the formula is a little more complex as labor, materials, and other costs incurred in production would also be added to beginning inventory with purchases before subtracting ending inventory.

Purchases

Purchases would include the actual prices paid—the invoice price less trade discounts—for goods to be sold or raw materials used in production. However, cash discounts received for paying early can be reported as income or a reduction to purchases, as long as you are consistent in your approach. Purchases would be reduced by any returns and allowances. Also, if any of the purchases are withdrawn for personal use, be sure to reduce purchases, as items used personally are not deductible and should not be included in the calculation of cost of goods sold.

Manufacturing Labor and Materials

For manufacturers, labor would include direct and indirect labor used in producing the raw materials into a finished product. Indirect labor costs would include salaries for production supervisors and wages for warehouse and packaging labor, as well as labor costs for any other workers indirectly involved in the production process. Materials and supplies used directly or indirectly in manufacturing goods would be included in costs of goods sold, but any materials and supplies not used in the manufacturing process should be deducted as ordinary business expenses.

HOW DO I TRACK INVENTORY AND COST OF GOODS SOLD?

Tracking inventory and costs is crucial for a business that makes or buys goods to sell. For tax planning purposes, you have to know what your taxable net income (or loss) is during the taxable year so that you can plan for the tax liability and make any needed adjustments before year-end. For business and cash flow purposes, you have to be able to monitor gross profit, inventory levels, and overhead costs on a consistent basis so that you can make informed decisions on future purchases and production. How well you manage inventory and cost information can have a big impact on your success as a business, so it is important that you spend time finding the best solution for tracking this information.

Using QuickBooks™ for Inventory

For the small businesses with a minimal amount of inventory items, the inventory option within QuickBooks works very well, at least as long as the data entry work is consistent with how Intuit® intended it, and time is spent on all the extra steps required. I have had to clean up many muddled QuickBooks files in my career and some of the worst were for companies that started using the inventory option, but then slowly stopped being consistent or took shortcuts on the data entry. If you are going to use QuickBooks to track your inventory, please understand that it takes a lot of upfront time to input and set up all your inventory items, and then extra input time for common transactions as you have to keep up the inventory information. Once you have the procedures down and you are consistent, the system works very well. In addition, QuickBooks allows you to assign costs to jobs with minimal data entry, so overall it is a good solution for most small businesses that are not manufacturers.

Other Inventory Tracking Solutions

For manufacturers or small businesses with larger inventories, separate inventory or job costing software may be needed. There are a wide variety of inventory software packages that integrate with accounting software like QuickBooks, but provide more tools and customization for managing larger inventories. For larger retail operations or manufacturers, there are complete accounting software packages that are robust and handle all areas of your business. Lastly, many wholesale and manufacturing businesses have custom software designed to meet their specific needs.

Regardless of the solution you choose, I would offer some caution based on my experiences with larger businesses and the software solutions.

- Be skeptical of complete, all-in-one accounting and business management software packages. While they are great solutions that can integrate every part of your business, they are costly to purchase and implement, the conversions take a long time, and you have to invest heavily into training and adaptation of your procedures to the established best practices.

- Custom software can be a good option if you find a good programmer who has a good understanding of the industry and accounting principles. The problem is that most programmers do not understand accounting, so often the custom software fails to provide correct cost and inventory information and only frustrates your tax professional.

- Development and implementation is a very difficult process, and I have seen custom software take over two years to be fully developed and implemented. Manage the conversion very closely and make sure there are clear deadlines for the developers and your manager employees.

- Finally, understand that even the best software solution is not going to solve all your problems. Software can provide valuable cost information and data, but if you do not have procedures in place and accountability in your organization to insure the information is used, then much of that value is wasted. Work with your tax professional to design procedures that will make the best use of the information from the software.

Chapter 4

BUSINESS DEDUCTIONS: WHAT, WHEN, AND HOW MUCH?

N ow that we have examined business income and cost of goods sold, it is time to turn our attention to the most popular section of most tax forms—the business deductions section. In fact, the most frequently asked questions from new business owners revolve around what can be deducted. This section will cover the foundational rules on deductions and summarize what is deductible and what is not. For detailed information on specific deductions, refer to Part III of this book entitled Maximizing Your Deductions.

WHAT CAN BE DEDUCTED?

Section 162(a) of the Internal Revenue Code gives business owners a basic rule to use in determining whether an expense qualifies as a business expense. To be deductible, a business expense must be:

- Incurred in connection with a trade or business,
- both ordinary and necessary for the business, and
- not lavish or extravagant under the circumstances.

If you look up the specific tax code, you will find that it does not define any of the above terms in much detail. However, based on a history of court cases on the matter, an "ordinary" expense is one that is common and acceptable in your industry, while a "necessary" expense is one that is helpful and appropriate for your business. The "lavish" and "extravagant" wording in Internal Revenue Code 162(a) is actually in regards to travel expenses, but the concept is often applied to all expenses as a common sense test that fits well with the concept of ordinary and necessary. After evaluating an expense based on your specific industry and business, you should look at your specific circumstances and make sure the expense is not out of proportion to your level of sales or structure.

You Can Be a Pig, Just Don't Be a Hog

If you have a hard time justifying an expense with a straight face and a short explanation, it is likely lavish or extravagant. The quote "pigs get fat, hogs go to slaughter" always comes to mind when looking at this issue, as most of the deductions I have seen the IRS disallow in audits have been expenses where the client went a little too far. Had they just taken a more reasonable approach and paid a little more in tax, they might have avoided the attention of the IRS altogether. Unfortunately, once the IRS finds an expense that is lavish and extravagant, they are quite efficient at opening up all open tax years and making an example out of you—so be a pig, just don't be a hog.

What Cannot Be Deducted?

Now that we have a general rule for what is deductible, we need to look at several items that are not deductible.

Expenses Already Used to Figure Cost of Goods Sold

In the previous chapter, we looked at the costs that make up cost of goods sold, as well as the businesses that are required to keep an inventory and calculate these costs on the tax return. These costs are a "deduction" in that they reduce gross receipts in the calculation of gross income. However, for IRS reporting purposes, these costs are not deductions that would be reported in the deduction section of business tax forms. In fact, the IRS stresses the importance of not duplicating expenses by deducting costs already included in the calculation of cost of goods sold. While this is less likely to happen if you use accounting software properly, it is a concern for smaller sole proprietorships with inventory who use a non-computerized accounting system—especially if they prepare their own tax returns. This can be a costly error, which is another reason why I strongly urge against self-preparing business tax returns.

Capital Expenditures

Not all expenditures can be deducted in full within the year of purchase. Items purchased that are materials in amounts that will last longer than one year have to be capitalized, which is an accounting term that basically means that the deduction is spread out over the useful life of the items. Examples would include equipment, furniture, buildings, and leasehold improvements. These capitalized items are called fixed assets, and I will discuss them in detail in chapter 5.

Personal Expenses

It should not come as a shock that personal expenses would not be deductible for a business; but it is something that the IRS looks very closely at, so it is important to understand the difference between personal and business expenses. First, any living or family expenses, like groceries or clothing, would clearly be personal and not deductible for a business. However, there are a number of expenses that are often used partly for business and partly for personal purposes, like vehicles, cell phones, and computers. The general rule in this case is that you would deduct the business portion of the expense. There are many special rules and countless exceptions, which are discussed in detail in Part III of this book, but the important point here is that you need to clearly separate personal expenses so that they are not included in with business deductions.

When Can the Deductions Be Taken?

For a business on the cash basis method of accounting, deductions are deductible when they are paid for, except for credit card charges, which are deductible when the charge is made and not when the credit card bill is paid.

For a business on the accrual basis of accounting, expenses are generally deductible when incurred or when the business becomes obligated for the expense. For more detailed information on the cash and accrual methods of accounting, refer to chapter 7.

How Much Can Be Deducted?

How much is too much? Well, it all comes back to how much is "ordinary and necessary" for your particular business and industry. For the main expenses required in your industry to sell your product or services, the IRS will rarely call the amounts into question. However, whenever personal use or enjoyment factors into an expense, expect the IRS to be pay close attention to the amounts deducted. Sometimes at year-end, you may even want to limit a deduction type if it turns out that it is out of proportion and might create a red flag.

In addition to the occasional self-imposed limitation on deductions to avoid the attention of the IRS, there are also IRS imposed limitations on certain deductions and losses. The most well known limitation is the 50 percent limitation on meals and entertainment, which is discussed in more detail in chapter 14. Net operating losses can be limited depending on income and carried forward, while pass-through losses from S corporations or partnerships can be limited by the shareholder's basis. Finally, some expenses like traffic fines and political contributions are completely non-deductible for tax purposes.

Chapter 5

FIXED ASSETS AND DEPRECIATION

Not all costs incurred in the operation of a business are fully deductible in the year of purchase. Generally, larger expenditures have to be deducted over a period of time determined by the property class of the expenditure. This creates a difference between net cash flow and net taxable income, which can result in surprise tax bills for small business owners who do not understand the rules on fixed assets. To make matters worse, the tax rules and limits on depreciation are constantly being changed by Congress, sometimes within the last few weeks of a tax year. It is very important that you not only understand the essential basics on fixed assets, but also that you work with your tax professional whenever you make a large fixed asset purchase so you understand the current rules and the impact the purchase will have on your business.

This chapter covers all the essentials on fixed assets that you need to understand, as well as overviews of the different depreciation elections and methods available. This practical information is foundational and will enable you to better understand how fixed asset purchases and disposals affect your taxable income, which will help you make wise investments in your business.

WHAT IS A FIXED ASSET?

Some small business tax books may use terms like "long term assets" or "capital expenses," but I think it is important that you use the same terminology as your tax professional, as it just makes communication easier. Tax law is confusing enough to explain as it is, so being on the same page with basic terminology definitely helps.

A fixed asset is an expenditure that is material in an amount that will last longer than one year. What is material for one business may not necessarily be the same for another business, but generally it would be around $200 to $500 for most small businesses. Items that would be used within a year, or do not have a useful life longer than one year, would not be classified as a fixed asset. For example, an Apple® iPad would be a fixed asset as it costs more than $500 and lasts longer than one year; but a wireless keyboard you purchased later to go with the iPad that only cost $40 would not necessarily be a fixed asset and could be deducted in full in the year of purchase as an office expense since it is not material in amount.

Keep in mind, these are only basic guidelines for determining what should be classified as a fixed asset. There are many exceptions and special rules, some of which we will discuss in this chapter, but again I would recommend talking with your tax professional before making any large purchases.

Common fixed asset categories include equipment, furniture, computers, software, vehicles, buildings, land, and leasehold improvements. There are also intangible assets, like goodwill, patents, and copyrights, which are material expenditures for assets without physical substance that are amortized over the life of the assets, which is usually fifteen years.

Accounting for Fixed Assets

Fixed asset purchases require more documentation than normal expenditures, and it is important to properly classify your purchases in your accounting system so that your tax professional does not have to hunt for them in your expense accounts. By following a few simple procedures, you will save time and money and ensure that all fixed assets are accounted for correctly on the tax return.

- Keep a file during the year to hold copies of invoices and documentation for any fixed asset purchases. At year-end, the contents of the file should be provided to your tax professional so that they can set up the fixed assets properly.

- When inputting purchases that qualify as fixed assets, make sure you post them to a fixed asset account and not to an expense account. At year-end or on a regular basis, reconcile your fixed asset account(s) to your file of fixed asset purchase invoices to make sure nothing has been misclassified.

- If a purchase includes several different fixed assets, make sure you input all the split details into your accounting system and use serial numbers if possible. Your tax professional has to input fixed asset purchases into their software individually and match up asset sales and disposals to prior year purchases, so detailed accounting records save time and will lower your tax prep bill.

- In the memo field of your fixed asset purchase transactions, indicate if the asset is new or used. Your tax preparer will thank you, as it will save them time in identifying purchases that qualify for bonus depreciation (more on this later).

- If you are unsure if a purchase qualifies as a fixed asset, post it to the fixed asset account anyway and your tax professional can reclassify the purchase if needed.

- If you purchase a large amount of tools or low cost equipment below the material limit for your business, you can create an expense account for them so that your tax professional can easily review the items you did not capitalize.

How Are Fixed Assets Deducted?

With the exception of special bonus depreciation and expensing elections, fixed assets are generally not deducted in the year of purchase. Instead, fixed assets are "capitalized", which means they become assets of the business rather than expenses, and their cost is spread out over a recovery period by means of depreciation or amortization expense. The expense would be taken each year until the full cost, or the business use portion, of the asset has been expensed.

For your accounting records and financial statements, the traditional book depreciation method is straight-line, which is calculated by claiming depreciation evenly over the useful life of the fixed asset. However, for tax purposes, there are many depreciation methods and special elections available, and the specific rules and limits have been changing so much lately that it is hard to keep track of when specific rules begin and when they expire. There are currently a number of generous depreciation rules that allow most purchases to be depreciated very quickly, if not all in the year of purchase; however, after 2012 most of these rules are scheduled to expire or be dramatically reduced. Since there is so much that is subject to change, this chapter will concentrate more on the methods and concepts than the actual limits.

WHEN DOES DEPRECIATION BEGIN?

Depreciation begins when a fixed asset is put into use. This is critical near year-end when business owners are buying fixed assets to lower taxable income. It is not enough to pay for them in advance or accrue the purchase—the fixed asset actually has to be received and put into use to be deducted, so be very careful with purchases near year-end.

How much "use" is required before year-end? Well, a perfect example near my hometown of Portland, OR, is the Trojan Nuclear Power Plant. While commercial operation of the plant did not start until May 1976, the operators fortunately achieved criticality on December 15, 1975, and then they hooked it up to the grid on December 23, 1975. So essentially they flipped the switch and used it briefly before year-end and then headed home for Christmas with depreciation on their books. Bottom line, even if the use is minimal before year-end, make sure the asset is actually put into use if you want the depreciation in the current tax year.

WHAT ASSETS CANNOT BE DEPRECIATED?

Other than fixed assets that have not been put into use, there are several other fixed assets that cannot be depreciated. In fact, land cannot be depreciated at all regardless of use or any other factor, and it basically stays on the books at cost until it is sold. Other non-depreciable assets include property placed in service and disposed in the same year, certain intangible assets, and property used only for personal activities.

WHAT IS THE SECTION 179 DEDUCTION?

The most popular and well-known special depreciation election is the Section 179 deduction. In fact, it is probably one of the only sections of the Internal Revenue Code that small business owners ever refer to, as it has become an important tool to minimize tax liability. If you are a new business owner, you might not be as familiar with the election, but basically it allows you to write off the entire cost of a qualifying fixed asset in the year of purchase as long it is within the allowed limits. While those limits change each year, the fundamentals of the deduction have remained the same.

What Property Qualifies?

In order to elect the Section 179 deduction, the property purchased must meet all of the following requirements:

- **The property must be acquired by purchase.** This means that if it is gifted or inherited property, it will not qualify. Also, if it was received in whole or part by trade, the portion that was received in trade does not qualify. Finally, if the property is acquired from a controlled group or related person, the property does not qualify.

- **The property must be "new to you."** In other words, the property can be used as long as the property is a new acquisition to your business. This is an important difference when compared to bonus depreciation, which we will cover in the next section.

- **The property must be acquired for business use.** To qualify, the property must be used in a trade or business and the business use has to be more than 50 percent in the year you put it in service.

- **It must be eligible property.** Generally, only tangible personal property is eligible for the deduction; however, there are many specific exceptions for certain other tangible property, as well as temporary exceptions for qualified real property, qualified leasehold improvements, and off-the-shelf software.

Excluded Property for 179 Depreciation

In addition to the above requirements, there are several types of property that the IRS specifically excludes from Section 179 depreciation. In general, excluded property includes: land and improvements, certain property leased to others, air conditioning and heating units, certain property used to furnish lodging, most property used outside the United States, property used by certain tax-exempt organization, and certain property used by governmental units or foreign persons or entities.

How Much Can Be Deducted?

After you have established that a fixed asset purchase qualifies for the 179 deduction, you have to determine the amount of the deduction that is allowed. The amount of Section 179 depreciation that can be deducted in the year of purchase depends on dollar limits which, in this recessionary economy, change each year, and more importantly—business income limits.

Dollar Limits

Section 179 deduction limits have been very generous in recent years, thanks to an eleventh hour round of stimulus in December 2010. For 2011, you could generally deduct up to $500k, and for 2012 this limit was reduced to $139k, which is still fairly generous. Unfortunately, unless Congress passes a new round of stimulus, their generosity fades in 2013 when the limit is reduced all the way down to $25k. Keep in mind, Congress will likely change this as 2013 gets closer.

The Section 179 deduction is intended for small businesses, as there is an upper limit imposed on larger businesses that can limit or eliminate the Section 179 deduction. The upper limit is based on the total cost of qualifying Section 179 property that you place into service in a tax year. For 2011, the upper limit phase-out began at $2,000,000, which was not much of a limit, but in 2012 it was reduced to

$560k. For 2013, it is scheduled to be reduced to $200k. Most small businesses do not have to worry about this limit as it is fairly large; however, if you have a year with a large amount of acquisitions, you might need to be aware of this limit.

Business Income Limits

In simple terms, you generally have to make a net profit in order to deduct Section 179 depreciation, and any amounts not allowed in a tax year are carried forward. While this rule is fairly complex and one that your tax professional calculates, you should be aware of the following issues related to the business income limit that can greatly impact your Section 179 deduction:

- The business income limit is based on net taxable income without regard to the Section 179 deduction, the self-employment tax deduction, any net operating carry back or carry forward, or any unreimbursed employee business expenses.

- For pass-through entities (partnership, LLC, LLP, or S corporation), the income limits apply at two levels—the entity level and the owner level. Basically, the entity calculates their deduction based on the entity income limit and allocates it to each of the owners. The owners then have to apply the income limit at their personal return level, which could be different for owners that have other sources of business income.

- In order to calculate the business income limit for S corporations, you have to add shareholder wages to net taxable income. Even though this makes calculations more complex, this is a great benefit to S corporation owners.

- If you are a passive owner in a partnership or S corporation, the Section 179 depreciation allocated to you is not deductible and is an adjustment to your basis.

Caution!

Owners of multiple pass-through entities need to be careful in their tax planning to make sure their flow-through Section 179 deductions do not exceed the income limit at their personal level—especially with dollar limits being reduced each year. Even though a Section 179 deduction may not exceed income limits at the entity level, the combined Section 179 deductions added together at the personal level may exceed the income limit. If you have the same tax professional handle both your entity and individual returns, this problem can be avoided as they can coordinate the income limits at both levels before deciding to use Section 179 depreciation.

There are additional complexities and special rules; however, as a business owner, this is all you really need to know. Your tax professional actually has to calculate everything and know all the intricate rules; you just need to be aware of the limits so that you can make solid asset purchase decisions and reasonably estimate net taxable income for the tax year.

Warning!

While the Section 179 deduction is a great tool to reduce your tax liability, make sure the fixed assets you are purchasing to get the deduction are actually needed by the business to increase capacity and profitability. Also, be very cautious if you are taking on debt to purchase the assets, as it can cause long-term cash flow problems despite the fact that it provides a current tax benefit.

What Is Bonus Depreciation?

Temporary acceleration provisions for depreciation have become commonplace since 2002, when Congress allowed businesses to claim "bonus" depreciation equal to 30 percent of the cost of new, qualifying purchases. Later in May 2003, President Bush signed into effect the Job and Growth Tax Relief Reconciliation Act that allowed 50 percent bonus depreciation. Since then, bonus depreciation has been turned on and off again by Congress throughout the years as needed to stimulate the economy. Each time, there are slightly different bonus allowances and timeframes; however, the basic elements of bonus depreciation have remained the same.

What Property Qualifies?

Unlike Section 179 depreciation rules, the following bonus depreciation rules are much more specific:

- It is only available for **new property**,
- only personal property and certain types of real property qualify (property referred to as Section 1245 property by the IRS), and
- the class life of the asset must generally be twenty years or less.

To qualify as new property, it must be brand-new from the factory and not just new to you. This is an important difference when compared to Section 179 depreciation, which can be applied to new and used fixed assets. Make sure you clearly identify new fixed assets in your records so that your tax preparer can take full advantage of bonus depreciation.

The IRS category of "Section 1245" property is actually a very broad category, and it is much easier to look at what property does not qualify under Section 1245:

- Buildings and other permanent structures,
- land and improvements,

- structural components of a building, and
- most intangible assets like goodwill and patents.

Most other fixed assets not included above qualify as Section 1245 property, and if they are new and have a class life of twenty years or less, they also qualify for bonus depreciation. This would include machinery and equipment, printing presses, gasoline storage tanks and pumps, grocery store counters, signs, and some land improvements like sidewalks, driveways, curbs, roads, parking lots, and drainage facilities. This gives incredible flexibility to a small business owner and provides great incentive to invest in an existing business or start a new one. However, all good things come to an end, so you may need to act quickly unless Washington makes additional extensions.

How Much Longer is Bonus Depreciation Available?

Based on current tax law as it exists at this time, the window for bonus depreciation is closing quickly, and based on the current gridlock and deficit woes, it is unlikely we will see much change to this schedule.

In 2010, we had 50 percent bonus depreciation until 9/28/10, which is when a new 100 percent bonus depreciation rule kicked in. Like an early morning door buster sale, the generous round of 100 percent bonus depreciation only lasted until 1/1/12 (except for certain longer-lived and transportation property). However, if you missed out, there is still 50 percent bonus depreciation available until 1/1/13. At that point, if Congress does not extend the rules, bonus depreciation will end and Section 179 depreciation will be the only means of getting first-year expensing of fixed assets.

State Issues with Bonus Depreciation

As you may be well aware, the federal government can rack up large deficits without balancing the budget and create stimulus tax bills that have not been paid for. States do not

---

Bonus Depreciation Example

A printing business buys a brand new printing press for $100k in 2012. If Section 179 depreciation is unavailable because of the dollar or business income limit, the press can be depreciated using bonus depreciation. The first year depreciation for the press would be 50 percent of the cost ($50k) plus normal depreciation on the cost less the bonus portion, which would be around $5,000. A deduction of $55k on a fixed asset costing $100k is still a great deduction even though it would have been $100k in 2011. However, if the company waits to invest in a new press until 2013, and if Section 179 is still unavailable, normal depreciation would only be about $10k. Even if Section 179 depreciation is available for the company in 2013, the limits for 179 are only $25k in 2013, so their first-year deduction will be much more limited than with a purchase in 2012.

---

have this luxury, and so many states struggling with their own budget problems had to "disconnect" from the new federal tax laws. In other words, many states do not allow the bonus depreciation that is available on the federal return and only allow normal depreciation that was available before the new federal laws. This translates to additions to state income if you claim bonus depreciation on the federal return, and sometimes these additions can be substantial and provide an unwelcome surprise tax bill for small business owners.

Be careful in planning for large purchases and have your tax professional project the effect of any state additions for you. The state tax laws are always changing, and some states that disconnected from new federal rules for a few years are even starting to reconnect to Federal bonus rules, so year-end tax planning is very important for small business owners at this point.

Caution!

It your corporation files tax returns based on a fiscal year, you need to understand an important difference between bonus and Section 179 depreciation. Bonus depreciation starts and expires upon specific dates, while Section 179 depreciation limits are based on tax years beginning in specific years. This means that fiscal year filers will get to take advantage of higher Section 179 depreciation limits after they have expired for calendar year filers. When planning large fixed asset purchases, make sure you are careful in estimating depreciation, as most information available is written for calendar year filers.

WHAT IS MACRS DEPRECIATION?

If you cannot use bonus or Section 179 depreciation on a fixed asset purchase, the default method of depreciation for tax purposes is the Modified Accelerated Cost Recovery System (MACRS). Under this system, the IRS has established property classes that group fixed assets based on recovery periods, which are intended to resemble the useful lives of the assets. For example, computer equipment would be classified as five-year property and be depreciated over a five-year recovery period. Below is a list of the different property classes and common fixed assets that fall into each class:

- **Three-year property**—semi-trailer trucks (tractors) and qualified rent-to-own property.

- **Five-year property**—computers, office equipment, and automobiles.

- **Seven-year property**—office furniture and non-office machinery and equipment.

- **Ten-year property**—water transportation equipment and single-purpose agricultural structures.

- **Fifteen-year property**—certain land improvements like fences, roads, and sidewalks.

- **Twenty-year property**—multi-purpose farm buildings and certain sewer property.

In addition to these groupings, there is also a twenty-five-year property group that only pertains to water utility property. Residential rental property is depreciated over twenty-seven-and-a-half years and it takes thirty-nine years to depreciate nonresidential real property.

MACRS Depreciation Tables

MACRS depreciation is calculated based on IRS tables, which list the allowable depreciation percentages for each year of a fixed asset's recovery period. The tables for property classes with recovery periods from three years to twenty years are listed below. Property classes with recovery periods over twenty years are depreciated using straight-line depreciation.

As you can see from the MACRS tables, the depreciation is accelerated for assets with shorter recovery periods. As you get closer to the twenty-year recovery period, the depreciation starts to resemble the straight-line depreciation method. As a small business owner, you do not need to know how to correctly calculate depreciation, but you should have a basic understanding of how long it will take to recover the cost of your fixed asset purchases. Your tax professional will calculate depreciation each year for you and provide you with a depreciation schedule, so just make sure you provide them with accurate fixed asset purchase and sale information.

Depreciation Rates By Property Class						
Year	3-year	5-year	7-year	10-year	15-year	20-year
1	33.33%	20.00%	14.29%	10.00%	5.00%	3.75%
2	44.45	32.00	24.49	18.00	9.50	7.22
3	14.81	19.20	17.49	14.40	8.55	6.68
4	7.41	11.52	12.49	11.52	7.70	6.18
5		11.52	8.93	9.22	6.93	5.71
6		5.76	8.92	7.37	6.23	5.29
7			8.93	6.55	5.90	4.89
8			4.46	6.55	5.90	4.52
9				6.56	5.91	4.46
10				6.55	5.90	4.46
11				3.28	5.91	4.46
12					5.90	4.46
13					5.91	4.46
14					5.90	4.46
15					5.91	4.46
16					2.95	4.46
17						4.46
18						4.46
19						4.46
20						4.46
21						2.23

SPECIAL CASES

There are several types of fixed assets that are treated differently or have special depreciation rules:

- **Software**—You would think that software would be depreciable over five years like computers, but it is actually amortized over three years. However, in recent years the Section 179 depreciation deduction has been available for off-the-shelf software.

- **Vehicles**—There are special rules when it comes to depreciating vehicles, which are covered in detail in chapter 12.

- **Leasehold improvements**—By default, lease-hold improvements are depreciable over thirty-nine years using straight-line depreciation; however, before 2012 there were incentives that allowed qualifying leasehold improvements to be depreciated over fifteen years, which meant business owners could use bonus or Section 179 depreciation if available. Even though most of the incentives have expired, 50 percent bonus depreciation is still available through 12/31/12, as qualified leasehold improvements are included in the definition of qualified property for bonus depreciation. You can claim the 50 percent of the cost of the improvement, but the rest has to be depreciated over thirty-nine years. If you think you may benefit from this incentive, make sure you meet with your tax professional to find out if your leasehold improvements qualify.

REPAIRS VS. IMPROVEMENT

It always seems that equipment breaks down at the most inopportune time in business, and the last thing you are probably thinking about when calling the repairperson is how the cost will be treated on your tax return. After all, you are likely more worried about the cost of the business interruption and potential lost revenue from the downtime, and rightfully so. However, after the dust settles and you receive the repair bill, you need to be aware of an important classification issue that can greatly impact your taxable income in the case of large overhauls.

In concept, a repair is an expense to keep an asset in efficient operating condition, while an improvement would be permanent betterment that materially increases the value or extends the useful life of the property. Unfortunately, when dealing with actual repair costs in small businesses, the line between a currently deductible repair and a capital expenditure that has to be depreciated is not always clear. You really have to review the larger repairs on a case-by-case basis and consider the facts and circumstances and underlying documentation. Also, watch for repairs that include upgrades or adaptations for new use, as this is generally a sure sign that the cost should be capitalized. Lastly, make sure you provide sufficient information on large repairs to your tax professional so that they can properly classify the costs. Granted, with all the generous depreciation rules right now, this is not that critical of an issue; however, as Section 179 limits are reduced and bonus depreciation goes away, it is something that small businesses will need to be cautious.

SALE, DISPOSALS, AND TRADE-INS

Up until this point, we have only discussed purchases of fixed assets, but eventually all fixed assets have to be sold, disposed, or traded-in. Unfortunately, many small business owners are often surprised by the tax impact of an asset sale or trade-in, as it is easy to forget about the depreciation taken on the fixed asset. In order to avoid unwelcome tax surprises, you should have a basic understanding of how sales, disposals, and trade-ins are taxed, and you need to make sure to contact your tax professional whenever such a transaction is being contemplated.

When you sell a fixed asset you are taxed on the difference between the selling price and your basis in the asset. The basis is calculated by deducting depreciation taken over the years from the original cost of the asset. If the fixed asset is fully depreciated, the calculation is simple and the taxable gain is the selling price since there is no remaining basis. Even if the fixed asset is not fully depreciated, the calculation is still fairly simple as long has you have a current depreciation schedule from your tax professional; but if a trade-in is involved, it can get much more complicated. Regardless of the situation, make sure you communicate with your tax professional on disposals and have them prepare the adjusting entry needed to properly record the disposal in your accounting records.

Chapter 6

DEDUCTING PAYMENTS TO WORKERS

Initially, many small, one-owner operated businesses can grow successfully without hiring help; however, eventually there is a point where further growth requires the help of subcontracted labor, employees, or a combination of the two. This can be a difficult transition for small business owners as the rules are a little complex unless you have prior training. Plus, it does not help that the payroll tax rates and credits are ever changing now that politicians seem to be favoring the use of the payroll tax system for passing through stimulus funds and other incentives. Nevertheless, it is essential that the small business owner clearly understands the rules on paying workers, as the risk of penalties, lawsuits, and fines is substantial in this area—even in cases of simple errors and negligence.

In addition to learning how to correctly classify workers, this chapter covers the basics of taxable compensation, payroll reporting, and payroll taxes. Even if you use a payroll service, this is important information as there are payroll taxes for which a business owner can be held personally liable.

How Should I Classify Payments to Workers?

How you classify payments to a worker for services is very important as it has significant tax implications for your business and the worker. You should carefully examine the relationship that exists—both in writing and in fact and circumstance—between your business and each worker providing services, and you should come to an agreement with each worker, so that there are no misunderstandings come tax time. Of the four classifications that a worker providing services can fall under, the independent contractor and employee classifications are the most common in small business, and therefore they will be the focus in this section.

Independent Contractor

Workers who offer their services to other businesses and the general public on a contract-basis are usually independent contractors. Common examples are consultants, self-employed professionals, freelancers, subcontractors, and other workers in independent trades and professions. While it remains a source of controversy with the IRS and state employment agencies, the general rule is that a worker is an independent contractor if the person hiring their services only has control over the result of the work and not the manner in which the work is completed.

Example

If you hired a website designer to create a new website for your business, you would likely direct the designer as to the type of site that you wanted, but you would not tell them what software to use, when to work on the website or where they need to perform the work. If the website designer is an independent contractor, then they would retain control over how, where, and when the work is done.

Common-Law Employee

If you have the right to control how, where, and when a worker performs work for your businesses, then the worker is likely an employee. It does not matter if you provide a free environment for your workers or label them as contract laborers, if the substance of the relationship indicates that an employee-employer relationship exists, the IRS and state employment departments will treat the worker as an employee. As an employer, you are generally required to withhold and pay income, social security, and Medicare taxes on wages paid to employees.

Employee vs. Independent Contractor

One of the most unclear and controversial tax topics for small business owners is the issue of whether a worker is an independent contractor or employee. This is due to the fact that there is no easy answer to the question, and every situation and industry is different, so there are no clear guidelines that can be used in all cases. Plus, it does not help that state employment departments and the IRS often use slightly different standards and methods when auditing this issue.

Each worker relationship needs to be evaluated carefully based on the unique facts and circumstances, as well as the elements of financial and behavioral control involved. Below

---

Employee vs. Independent Contractor Checklist

This is not an all-inclusive checklist, but a brief guide that will help you consider the many different factors involved in classifying a worker.

- **Instructions**—is the worker required to comply with instructions about when, where and how to perform work? The right to instruct a worker generally indicates that the worker is an employee.

- **Training**—is the worker required to train with experienced workers or attend training meetings? Training indicates control over how the work is done, which would point to classification as an employee.

- **Evaluation**—is there an evaluation system in place that measures not only the end result, but also how the work is performed? If such evaluation were in place, this factor would indicate the worker is likely an employee.

- **Length of Relationship**—was the worker hired for a specific project or time frame? Such terms are typical of contracts with independent contractors, but employee relationships are usually expected to continue indefinitely.

- **Availability of Services**—are the worker's services available to the general public? Independent contractors typically provide services to other businesses, advertise and maintain a business location.

- **Unreimbursed Expenses**—does your business expect the worker to pay for their expenses and equipment? Independent contractor relationships usually involve a fair amount of unreimbursed expenses, while employees are typically reimbursed for expenses—especially with regards to fixed, recurring expenses.

- **Employee Benefits**—is the worker offered benefits like health insurance, paid vacation and sick time, or dependent care assistance? Businesses rarely offer these benefits to independent contractors, and usually the presence of such benefits would indicate an employer-employee relationship.

is a checklist that can be used when classifying a worker, which can help you avoid costly misclassifications that can result in additional tax, penalties, and interest.

What Are the Risks of Misclassification of Workers?

The consequences involved with misclassifying a worker can be fairly severe, and often the taxes, penalties, and interest resulting from workers being reclassified as employees are enough to bankrupt a business. Not only will you owe all the employment taxes that should have been paid on the payments to the worker, but they will also assess substantial penalties and interest—especially if they are auditing a tax year that is two or three years previous. Even worse, a reclassification can create major problems for the employee benefit plans that your business offers, and often it can even result in back benefits being owed to the reclassified workers.

State employment departments are much more likely to audit your business on this issue, and unfortunately, they are often much more zealous about the issue than IRS auditors. I have witnessed quite a few state employment department audits over the years, and they can be a very lengthy and painful process involving a large amount of documentation requests, interviews with your employees and independent contractors, and in-depth reviews of your procedures and policies. Often these audits are random; however, many of them are prompted by independent contractors trying to claim unemployment. This is why it is absolutely essential that your worker understands their classification and there is a written agreement to that fact.

How Can I Protect My Business From Worker Misclassification?

There are number of steps you can take to protect your business and reduce the risk of worker reclassification in an audit situation. You should regularly review all of your independent contractor relationships and make sure all the following steps have been taken.

- Have all independent contractors complete and sign Form W-9, Request for Taxpayer Identification Number and Certification, and keep the forms on file.

- Draft contracts or other written agreements for your independent contractors to sign and meet with them to make sure they understand the terms of the agreement.

- Make sure they are issuing invoices or billings to you, like any other business would send you, and that you are paying them accordingly.

- Make sure a significant portion of your industry treats similar workers as independent contractors. If it is a unique position, have your tax professional search for a court case that would support your classification.

- If the independent contractor has an unincorporated business and you paid them more than $600 for services in the calendar year, be sure to issue a 1099-MISC to them and the IRS after year-end.

Recent Development

The Small Business Jobs Act of 2010 has substantially increased the penalties for failing to timely file 1099-MISC forms. If you intentionally disregard sending these forms to vendors and the IRS, the penalty can be $500 per form. If you make an attempt by sending 1099-MISC forms and you miss some, the penalty goes down to $200 per form. Hopefully that is enough motivation for you to carefully go through your records at year-end to make sure you find all vendors eligible for a 1099-MISC and file them timely.

Do I Need an Employer Identification Number?

All employers are required to obtain a federal Employer Identification Number (EIN). If you are starting a new business that will have employees, the most expedient method to get an EIN is to go to www.IRS.gov and follow the link from the main page entitled "Apply for an Employer Identification Number (EIN) Online." From there you can follow their instructions and in ten minutes or less you will be issued an EIN. Alternatively, you can call 1-800-829-4933 and the IRS will take the information and issue you an EIN. If you are more comfortable with paper, you can download Form SS-4 and send it by fax or mail; however, using these methods will mean that you will have to wait for your EIN to be faxed or mailed to you.

If your existing business is structured as a corporation or partnership, you already have an EIN. However, if you have a sole proprietorship, an EIN is really only required if you are an employer or you have had to file excise tax returns.

What Is Taxable Employee Compensation?

Generally, all pay you give to an employee for services performed is subject to federal employment taxes. It may be in cash, paid by check, the taxable portion of fringe benefits, or the value of tangible goods given to the employee. Even that Christmas bonus you gave to each employee in cash is taxable compensation that needs to be reported if you want the deduction on the tax return.

It is critical to make sure all payments to your employees are reported on a paycheck. If you use a payroll processing service, all draws, bonuses, commissions, and any other similar payments need to be provided to them so that the payroll is correct. There is nothing worse than preparing a tax return for a business and finding bonus checks, wage settlements, or holiday gift checks that were not provided to the payroll processing company. Granted, corrections and adjustments can be made, but it can be very costly due to the large penalties involved with underreporting payroll and the complexity of amending payroll tax filings. Plus, employees normally file early in the year, so your error could also cost your employee additional tax preparation fees to amend, as well as penalties and interest on any tax due. It is definitely easier and less costly if you have it done right the first time, which can be done if you communicate thoroughly with your payroll processing company and have a clear understanding of what is, and what is not, taxable employee compensation.

What Forms of Employee Compensation Are Not Taxable?

There are a number of forms of employee compensation that are not taxable or reportable as wages. Other than non-taxable fringe benefits, the following items are common forms of compensation that clients ask about that are not taxable to employees.

Small Gifts to Employees

Small gifts that you give to your employees totaling less than $25 per year are not included as taxable wages to your employees and are deductible business expenses. Granted, this is a very small amount, but it should be enough to cover a small holiday gift. Keep in mind that these gifts cannot be made in cash or gift certificates, as they would be taxable at any amount.

Employee Awards

Employee awards can be tax-free to the employee and deductible by the business as long as they meet IRS rules and fall into one of three categories below and are within the deduction limits.

- **Achievement award**—this would be an award for length of service or a safety achievement that is awarded as part of a meaningful presentation, and is not awarded in a way that creates a significant likelihood of disguised pay. In order to be tax-free to the employee, it must be tangible personal property and not cash or check.

- **Length-of-service award**—the IRS gets a little picky on what qualifies for length-of-service. The employee must have completed at least five years of employment. Also, for long-time employees with more than five years of employment, you cannot give them another length-of-service award if they received one during the same year or in any of the prior four years.

- **Safety achievement awards**—a safety award is tax-free to the employee unless it is given to a manager, administrator, clerical employee, or other professional employee, which makes sense given that the only threat to these employees is the occasional paper cut. However, the IRS would not leave it that simplistic, so an additional restriction states that more than 10 percent of all employees (except for those listed above) cannot receive a safety achievement award in the same year (other than one of very small value).

In addition to the above rules, employee awards are limited to $400 per employee each tax year or $1,600 for all awards, whether or not they were made under a qualified plan, which is an established written plan or program that does not favor highly compensated employees. According to the rules, "highly compensated" is defined as employees who were 5 percent owners at any time during the year or preceding year, or received more than $110,000 in pay in the preceding year. For more information on achievement awards, refer to the *Employees' Pay* section of IRS Publication 535 *Business Expenses*.

Expense Reimbursements

If you directly reimburse an employee for substantiated expenses under an accountable plan, the reimbursement is not taxable compensation and the payment should be clearly posted to the related expense account and not a wage account. On the other hand, if your business has a non-accountable expense reimbursement plan, the expense advances are treated as taxable employee compensation. Generally, you have a non-accountable plan if:

- your employees are not required to timely substantiate expenses,

- you advance funds to your employee with no requirements regarding the return of excess funds,

- you advance or pay an amount to your employee regardless of whether you expect them to incur business expenses, and/or

- you pay an amount as reimbursement that would have otherwise been paid as wages.

Draws and Advances

Short-term loans to employees or regular draws paid in between long pay periods are not taxable compensation to employees. This is normally a straightforward issue; however, some businesses that use a monthly pay period, and process payroll through a large payroll processing company, choose to pay a regular draw to some employees because of the large cost that would be incurred for an additional payroll run. In this type of scenario, employees can get confused if the draws are consistent and direct deposited like the paychecks, and occasionally it can cause year-end tax issues, so be sure that your employee handbook clearly distinguishes draws from payroll. Also, keep in mind as the business owner that a draw is a temporary advance and not deductible until the payroll is actually paid.

When Is Payroll Reported and Deducted?

There is often some confusion over the timing of payroll reporting and deduction among small business owners, and much of that confusion comes from the fact that there are so many different dates involved in the payroll process including:

- pay period beginning and end dates,
- time card due dates,
- payroll processing dates (often called the payroll run date), and
- the actual pay day (date on paychecks).

Of all the different dates, the date on the paychecks is the most important, as it is on this date that the payroll is deducted for income tax purposes and the liability date for payroll tax purposes. For example, if a pay period ends 12/28/12 and the pay date is not until 1/4/13, the payroll run is reported on the first quarter 2013 quarterly payroll tax reports and the wage and tax deduction for a cash basis business cannot be taken until 2013.

This concept of when payroll is reported is very important at year-end as it can cause headaches for small business employers. If an employee is trying to catch-up their 401k or

SIMPLE IRA deferral so that they can reach the maximum contribution for the year, and the employer is not paying attention to the pay date at year end, an opportunity could be lost for the employee to reach the maximum contribution. Also, if an employer is not paying attention to pay dates, payroll tax deposits can be coded to the wrong quarter, which is a hassle to straighten out with the IRS or a state agency.

WHICH PAYROLL TAXES
ARE EMPLOYERS SUBJECT TO?

Even if you use a payroll service to prepare your payroll, you need to understand the different payroll taxes that are owed on the wages you pay to your employees. Not only is it important from a budgeting standpoint in calculating the true cost of employees, but it is also essential to understand since business owners can be held personally liable for some of the taxes that need to be remitted to the IRS.

Employer Payroll Taxes
The following taxes are paid by the employer and are an expense to a business:

- **Social Security Tax**—for 2012, the employer portion of Social Security tax is currently set at 6.2% of subject wages up to $110,100. Tax legislation has been proposed to lower this rate, and the wage limit is always increasing, so it is important to keep current on the rates and limits.

- **Medicare**—the employer portion of Medicare is 1.45% of subject wages and there is no maximum wage limit.

- **Federal Unemployment Tax (FUTA)**—up until recently, the FUTA tax rate was 0.8% on the first $7,000 paid to employees for most employers that timely pay qualifying state unemployment tax. However, Congress let a 0.2% surtax expire, so as of 7/1/11 the rate was reduced to 0.6%. There are also proposals to raise the limit to the first $15,000 of wages, so make sure you keep current if you are preparing payroll manually.

- **State Unemployment Tax**—every state unemployment tax system is different, but most states have much higher unemployment tax rates and wage limits than the FUTA tax. There are also many special rules for what is subject to the tax and how business owners can be exempt from the tax.

- **Other State Payroll Taxes**—states have a variety of additional taxes based on taxable wages including transit taxes and assessments based on the number of hours worked.

Employee Withholdings

The following taxes are withheld from employee wages and later remitted to federal and state tax agencies:

- **Federal and State Income Taxes**—income tax is withheld from an employee's wages in accordance with the exemptions and status claimed on their Form W-4 and the withholding tables.

- **Employee Social Security Tax**—for many years the tax rate of 6.2% stayed constant even though the wage limit was constantly adjusted upward, but in 2011, the rate was reduced to 4.2%. In 2012, the rate is 4.2% and the wage limit is $110,100.

- **Employee Medicare Tax**—like the employer portion, the employee portion of Medicare is 1.45% with no maximum wage limit.

- **Other State/Local Employee Taxes**—there are a variety minor state and local taxes that employees are subject to that have to be remitted to the taxing agencies.

Employee Withholdings and Personal Liability

Employee withholdings are considered "trust funds" as they are taxes that you hold in trust and then remit to the taxing agencies for your employees. It turns out that the IRS takes trust fund responsibility very seriously—so much that they can assess a penalty that is 100 percent of the unpaid trust fund taxes, named the Trust Fund Recovery Penalty, on responsible parties that acted willfully in not remitting the employee withholdings to the IRS. This responsible person can be an officer, employee, partner, accountant, director, or anyone else who has authority to sign checks and disburse business funds.

A penalty equal to 100 percent of the unpaid tax may seem severe—especially if you are a non-owner employee or manager—but the IRS actually has very good reason for such a stern response. If you are paying employees a stated wage, withholding taxes from that wage, and then not remitting those taxes to the taxing agencies, you are essentially committing fraud and not truly paying the stated wage you agreed to, which is unfair to all your competitors who are paying all their payroll taxes. It makes sense that the IRS agents handling this issue make unannounced visits to the business locations of offenders and even shut down businesses that are not able to get current after initial warnings. I have witnessed such visits many times in my career, and it is a very serious issue, so if you take anything from this book, make sure you stay current on your payroll deposits.

WHEN ARE PAYROLL TAX DEPOSITS DUE?

Now that you understand the importance of making payroll tax deposits, you need to know when the deposits must be made. That answer largely depends on the amount of your total Form 941 federal payroll tax liability, which is the sum of your federal employee withholdings, employee and employer social security tax, and employee and employer Medicare tax. For most small businesses, there are three possible schedules for paying payroll tax to the IRS.

Quarterly
If your business has a small level of payroll and your total Form 941 federal payroll tax liability is less than $2,500 in a quarter, then your payroll tax is paid with the quarterly tax return, which is due by the end of the month following the end of the quarter.

Monthly
Once your total Form 941 federal payroll tax liability exceeds $2,500 for the quarter; you need to start depositing monthly. After month-end, calculate the total Form 941 federal payroll tax liability amount and deposit the tax by the fifteenth of the following month.

Semiweekly
If your federal payroll tax liability on Form 941 starts to exceed $50,000 per year, you will likely receive a letter from the IRS stating that you are now a semiweekly depositor. Congratulations—you are now part of special group of employers that has to deposit payroll taxes on a semiweekly schedule, which is a very confusing schedule that only gives

you days to deposit your liability. The depositing rules are summarized in the table below, which you can refer to when determining deposit due dates. You may want to consider using a payroll preparation service unless you have an experienced bookkeeper on staff. The penalties that can result from late deposits or insufficient deposits can be substantial.

Semiweekly Deposit Schedule

If the Payday falls on a...	Then deposit taxes by the following...
Wednesday, Thursday, and/or Friday	Wednesday
Saturday, Sunday, Monday, and/or Tuesday	Friday

State Deposits

State depositing rules are often matched to your federal requirements, so make sure you are consistent. Also, check with your state to find out when each type of state tax is due. Employee withholdings are often due when federal deposits are due, and state employer taxes, like unemployment tax or transit taxes, are usually due quarterly.

FUTA Deposits

Federal unemployment tax (FUTA) deposits are paid quarterly, but only when your total accumulated FUTA liability reaches $500 or more. If your liability never exceeds this amount, the tax is paid with the annual Form 940.

WHAT PAYROLL TAX REPORTS ARE REQUIRED?

Even if a payroll service or tax professional prepares your quarterly and year-end payroll tax reports, you should still be familiar with the reports—especially if you are the owner who is signing the reports.

Quarterly Payroll Tax Reports

The primary federal payroll tax report is Form 941, which is due by the last day of the month following the quarter-end. The Form 941 reports the total wages, federal withholdings, social security tax, and Medicare tax for the quarter. Most states also have at least one quarterly payroll tax filing to report unemployment tax, withholdings, and any other state payroll taxes.

Year-End Reports

The federal Form 940, which reports wages subject to the Federal Unemployment Tax (FUTA), is due by January 31 of the following year. Employers with FUTA liability of less than $500 would finally pay their liability for the year with this form, while employers who already deposit monthly would simply report subject wages. Form W-3 and the W-2s are also due after year-end, with the W-2s due to the employees on January 31 and the Social Security Administration copies due by the end of February, although e-filing employers get an extended deadline of April 2. Many states have year-end reconciliation reports due by January 31 as well.

Lastly, as I mentioned earlier in our discussion on independent contractors, make sure you file Form 1099-MISC for any unincorporated contractors that you paid more than $600 to for services in the calendar year. The recipient copy is due January 31 and the IRS copy is due by the end of February.

Chapter 7

ACCOUNTING: THE KEY TO TAX SAVINGS & SUCCESS

Owning a small business is exciting and it is easy to spend countless hours passionately pursuing your goals and growing the business. Working on accounting records, on the other hand, is a painful task that many business owners put off as long as they can. Granted, donning the green visor and inputting transactions or reconciling a bank statement is anything but exciting; however, your accounting records and how you have them organized can have a huge impact on your tax savings, your business decisions, and ultimately the success of your business.

This chapter provides an overview of the essential accounting basics that small business owners need to understand, as well as practical steps you can take to ensure that your accounting records provide the proper foundation for your business. Much of the following advice comes from my years in public accounting, cleaning up disasters created by business owners who did not acquire an understanding of accounting basics or spend the time and money to set up an accounting system that provided them with good information. Even if you have a good accounting system in place and a competent accountant, this chapter will be a good review and you might even find ideas for improving your accounting records.

WHY IS ACCOUNTING IMPORTANT?

For starters, Internal Revenue Code §6001 requires a taxpayer to maintain adequate books and records to substantiate income, deductions, and credits, which means good accounting records are foundational if you want your reported income and deductions to weather an IRS audit. This is simple enough, but unfortunately—like commuters on a long, open stretch of road with no speed traps—many busy small business owners begin to overlook this basic rule of the road in their rush to meet all the other pressing demands of their business. In addition, many small business owners concentrate far too much energy on taking advantage of tax deductions while spending very little time on their record-keeping, which is a dangerous combination. You may have found an amazing tax strategy and tailored it to your exact circumstances with hours of tax planning; however, it will all be in vain if you keep poor records and cannot properly defend your position or deductions to the IRS.

Disallowance of tax deductions in an IRS audit can be very costly, but it is nowhere near the impact that poor accounting records can have on your business decisions. Running a business without timely and organized accounting records after too long usually results in cash flow problems, overuse of debt, missed opportunities, poor financial decisions, and surprise tax bills. Even worse, if you are delegating bookkeeping responsibilities to an employee or contract bookkeeper and not carefully monitoring the financial statements, you could end up paying some large penalties for late payroll tax deposits or miss catching the warnings signs of embezzlement and fraud, which unfortunately happens far too often in small businesses.

You may think I am a little dramatic, or even slightly biased since I make a living providing tax and accounting services, but I have witnessed far too many small business owners run into tax and cash flow problems because their accounting system was a mess, so I cannot stress enough the importance of proper accounting.

THE ESSENTIAL ACCOUNTING BASICS

Let's start with the accounting basics that you need to know as a business owner by walking through the process of accounting.

- **Recording**—Accounting begins at the transaction level with the recording of individual transactions. Every transaction is recorded in an accounting system and is posted to a system of accounts—often referred to as a chart of accounts.

- **Summarizing**—In a manual accounting system, this is a tedious process of adding columns of transactions and calculating balances; however, in computerized accounting systems, much of the summarizing occurs automatically. Summarizing also involves the reconciling of account details and making corrections and reclassifications so that the balances are correct.

- **Reporting**—Once the account balances are calculated and reconciled, the data is organized into standard accounting reports and financial statements. The most common statements are the balance sheet, income statement, and statement of cash flows, which can be generated instantly in a computerized accounting system.

- **Analyzing**—While small business owners generally keep a good handle on managing cash flow, most do not spend enough time reviewing the financial statements produced by their software. Reviewing financial statements in detail and comparing the data to prior periods is crucial, as it not only helps the business owner connect cash flow with profitability, but it also allows them to review trends and make projections that can be used in everyday business decisions.

Now that you have the big picture of the accounting process, it is important to understand the basic concepts and methods that are fundamental to accounting.

WHAT IS AN ACCOUNTING SYSTEM?

An accounting system is simply your overall organization of manual and computerized accounting solutions, procedures, and controls that together enable you to effectively complete the accounting process on a timely basis. Every business is different and accounting systems vary widely from business to business, so it is important to find effective solutions, procedures, and controls that fit your specific business and circumstances. Once it is set up and in place, the larger challenge is keeping current on the accounting work, staying organized, and making sure the procedures are followed consistently.

One of the foundations of an accounting system is the customized list of accounts that you post transactions to, commonly referred to as the chart of accounts. The chart includes asset, liability, equity, income, and expense accounts. Your list of accounts can be short and simple, or it can be complex with account numbers, sub-accounts, and departmentalization. It all depends on your business and reporting needed; however, how your chart is set up can greatly simplify or complicate your bookkeeping.

What Are Accounting Methods?

An accounting method is a set of rules that determine when you report income and expenses, and unfortunately there is more than one method to the madness that is accounting. The two most commonly used methods used in small businesses are the cash and accrual methods, but there are also hybrid and special accounting methods used by businesses with unique circumstances, which are basically variations of the cash and accrual methods. It is important that you understand the differences between cash basis and accrual basis. Not only will it make it easier to communicate with your tax professional, but you will also have a better grasp on when income and deductions will be reported for tax purposes. After all, only knowing what to report as income and deductions does not do you much good if you do not also know when they are deductible—especially at year-end when a simple misunderstanding of these basic concepts can sometimes amount to thousands of dollars in unexpected taxes.

Those of you who use accounting software like QuickBooks or Peachtree® may be wondering why this understanding of accounting methods is so important. After all, the software actually allows you to the change the accounting method used on the financial statements with the simple click of a button. This is a good point, as technology like this can save us a lot of time; however, in this case the technology only works correctly if the underlying transaction data is input correctly and as intended by the software designer. All it takes is a payment dated before an invoice at year-end or an unapplied customer payment and your automatically generated cash basis statements in QuickBooks will be incorrect, so automatic accounting basis conversions cannot always be trusted and require some manual review. As a small business owner, you should be able to recognize these errors and make corrections so that your books give you an accurate picture of net taxable income.

WHEN IS AN ACCOUNTING METHOD SELECTED?

The IRS allows you to select a method of accounting for tax purposes when you file the first tax return for your business, and sometimes is it not much a choice as some businesses are required to use the accrual method because of their industry or a combination of their gross sales and entity type. Generally, most businesses with average gross income under five million dollars can use the cash basis method, but once over five million, C corporations, partnerships with a C corporation as a partner, and businesses in manufacturing, wholesaling, retail, publishing, or sound recording have to use the accrual method. All businesses with average gross income over ten million have to use the accrual method. Make sure you know what accounting method your business uses for tax purposes and why the decision was made.

THE CASH BASIS METHOD

The cash basis of accounting is probably the most natural and intuitive method of accounting for income and deductions. The basic premise is that income is not recorded until the actual payment is received and deduction does not occur until the payment is actually made. Think of a checkbook register—like the one your mother (or grandmother) used meticulously to keep a current bank balance long before the days of credit cards and personal finance software. To keep an accurate balance in a register, you only record checks written and deposits taken to the bank. The cash basis method uses the same principle; however, in a business environment we need to keep track of income, expenses, and changes to balance sheet accounts in addition to simply balancing a checking account.

Cash Basis at the Transaction Level

Now let's go beyond the conceptual level to practical application and look at what the cash basis method looks like at the transaction level.

- **Income**—as stated earlier, income is not recorded until payment is received, so only cash sales and received payments on invoices would be included in income.

- **Expenses**—only paid bills and checks written can be deducted. The only exception is credit card charges, which are deductible when the charges are made and not when the credit card bills are paid.

- **Accounts Receivable and Accounts Payable**—both of these balances should be zero on the cash basis. Occasionally, accounting software can show negative balances on cash basis for these accounts, but usually this is the result of date or input errors.

- **Payroll Tax Liabilities**—technically only employee withholdings can be reported as payroll tax liabilities under cash basis. Any employer tax liabilities would need to be reversed.

When keeping accounting records under the cash basis method, it is crucial that dates are input correctly, especially near year-end. It is also important to reconcile bank and credit card accounts closely so that stale checks and erroneous entries are voided.

The Accrual Basis Method

Unlike the simplicity of the cash basis method, accrual basis is fairly complex and can be confusing unless you have taken financial accounting courses. Even though the ultimate aim of the accrual method is the matching of income and expenses, its rules do not come naturally for most small business owners. Under accrual accounting, income is recognized when earned and expenses are recorded when they are incurred. The recognition of income and expenses has nothing to do with actual payments and when they are received or paid, but instead the focus is on the timing of the events initiating the income or expense. Basically, if all the events required to earn the income or be obligated for an expense have happened, you record the income or expense.

Accrual Basis Accounting

What does this look like on a practical level for a business? Well, first of all, the accrual method requires many month and year-end adjusting journal entries, so you should definitely make sure you have a good accountant employed. In addition, there are many additional procedures that will need to be set up in your accounting system to insure that the financial statements are correctly stated under the accrual basis method.

- Your accounting system has to track accounts receivable much more closely, and you need to review delinquent balances regularly for accounts that need to be written off.

- Accounts payable has to be tracked and reconciled under the accrual basis, which will increase the data entry required in your accounting system. Your tax professional can shortcut this at year-end and calculate accounts payable based on the January expenses, but even then it requires much more work than reporting under the cash basis method.

- Accounting for insurance and taxes also requires much more data entry and reconciliation than under the cash basis method as you have to calculate prepaid and accrued balances at the reporting date. This requires an experienced accountant, as the accounting software will not calculate the prepaid and accrual amounts automatically.

- There are also many other prepaid and accrual balances that have to be reconciled and calculated at month and year-end.

CAN I CHANGE ACCOUNTING METHODS?

Now that you have a good understanding of the cash and accrual basis methods, some of you may be wondering why you are on the accrual basis. Well, often there are good reasons for choosing accrual basis when you are not required to use it; however, sometimes it is just the result of a misunderstanding of the rules on your tax professional's part or just an uninformed decision on your part. In either case, there is an option available that allows your business to change to the cash basis method, and in most cases, reduce your current year tax liability. The process involves Form 3115 and some complex calculations to ascertain the net adjustment resulting from the change, so you will definitely need to discuss it with your tax professional first. If it makes sense for your business, they can complete the form and calculations when they complete your next tax return.

AVOID TAX REPORTING OVER-COMPLICATION

If you have a new partnership or corporation that will soon be filing for the first time, you need to be aware of an important decision that your tax professional will be making that could over-complicate your tax return and cost you hundreds of dollars for unnecessary work each year. Basically, even though your business may report income and expenses on the cash basis, your tax professional has the option of reporting your balance sheet on Schedule L of your return on the accrual basis. If you have compiled or reviewed financial statements prepared annually, or if you have a larger company and an internal CPA or experienced accountant on staff, then this may make sense. However, if you do not need annual financial statements and you essentially use cash basis financial statements internally, then make sure your tax professional does not report the balance sheet on Schedule L on the accrual basis.

While preparing Schedule L on accrual basis for cash basis taxpayers may be the formal and traditional way to prepare the tax return, it requires your tax professional to prepare an accrual to cash calculation and complicates the rest of tax return, which translates to higher tax preparation fees and returns that are more difficult to understand. Plus, now that we have software that can instantly change financial statement data from accrual to cash basis, the formality and tradition is a little irrelevant.

How Should I Keep My Records?

Fortunately, the IRS does not have a required, uniform format for business records. As long as the business records are accurate and provide a clear representation of the business income and expenses, then there is a great deal of flexibility given to business owners in how they set up and keep their records. This flexibility has produced a wide variety of both manual and computer accounting systems among small businesses, so what should you use for your business?

How Not to Keep Your Records
Well, for starters we should discuss accounting systems that you should not use. Here, in no particular order, are the five worst accounting systems that I have come across in my twelve years in public accounting:

- **The shoebox accounting system**—this is a great idea if you want an extremely high bill from your tax professional. For the best results, have the receipts wrinkled up and mixed in no particular order, add random pictures of your pet or a recent vacation, and make sure you include some receipts from different years just to keep your tax professional on their toes.

- **The handwritten, single-page summary of income and expenses**—nothing instills confidence in a tax professional like a list of income and expenses with no backup or that resembles a grocery list—especially when all the numbers are conveniently rounded.

- **Saving twelve months of banks statements for your tax professional**—this is not really even an accounting system, but you would be surprised how many clients save twelve months of accounting input and reconciliation work for their tax professionals to complete during tax season. This is a good system if you enjoy finding a new tax professional each year.

- **The "is it personal or business?" accounting system**—mixing your personal and business transactions in a personal finance software file is another winner with tax professionals as it creates hours of never ending trivia.

- **The "good intentions" accounting system**—this disaster is often the result of an owner who bought a popular accounting software package with the great intention of getting training and assistance, but in the end just quickly input all the transactions and posted them haphazardly, leaving a big mess for their tax professional to sort out.

Hopefully you get the point from these examples—an accounting system has to be organized, detailed, accurate, and timely. This is can be done manually, with computers, or a mix of the two.

Manual Accounting Systems

Non-computerized accounting systems are becoming more and more uncommon in small businesses as technology continues to offer more accessible, time-saving solutions for accounting and bookkeeping. In addition, new devices have changed how and when data can be input, reviewed, and shared with others. Despite these advances, there are still some businesses that can benefit from a manual system— namely those with low transaction volume, no inventory, consistent monthly expenses, and few customers. Typical examples would be rental property owners, independent contractors, and small home-based businesses.

The most common manual systems utilize multiple long, columnar paper ledger sheets to record transactions. Separate ledger sheets are kept for each part of the business including cash receipts, cash disbursements, and payroll, then each are transferred onto one general ledger that combines all the information. The columns of the ledgers are used to track and total categories of income, expenses, and other deductions or withholdings. When you get to the end of a sheet, the columns are totaled and then carried forward to the next sheet, so it is important to double check your totals so that errors are not carried forward. Otherwise, the ledger sheets are fairly straightforward to fill out and can be customized to meet the needs of the business without too much work.

Overall, a manual system is more time-consuming— especially for someone who is tech savvy and knows that these repetitive tasks and manual calculations could be done by software. However, it is a very low cost solution and there is very little setup required when compared to using an accounting software package. If a manual accounting system fits your business type and you are more comfortable with a pen and paper than a computer, then you might consider the manual option. However, I would imagine that a large majority of small business owners would prefer to use accounting software for their businesses.

Computerized Accounting Systems

I have spent a significant portion of my career consulting and training small business clients on accounting software packages, which have become much more advanced over the last twelve years. However, even with all the great advancements and time-saving automations, accounting software is, at its core, largely based on the manual accounting system. QuickBooks is undoubtedly the most popular small business accounting software package on the market, and this is due largely to the fact that they took familiar elements of the manual accounting system and made software that was easy to learn and easy to input data. This ease of use has its drawbacks as new business owners who are untrained in QuickBooks or accounting can make quite a mess for their tax professional with the software. Nonetheless, computerized accounting systems are great tools and excellent timesavers for business owners, and it is only a matter of time before manual accounting and the green ledger sheets become a thing of the past.

Computerized Accounting Options

There are several varieties of computerized accounting systems used by small business owners, and each business owner should use a solution that best suits their needs.

- **QuickBooks and Peachtree**—both of these accounting software packages are very similar and offer the all-in-one solution for the small business owner. They are complete accounting systems and can handle just about any small business scenario if customized and set up correctly.

- **Microsoft® Excel**—some micro-businesses with low transaction volumes are candidates for simplified accounting systems using Microsoft Excel. Engineers are notorious for designing custom ledger systems in Excel.

- **Quicken, Microsoft Money®, and other personal finance software**—Occasionally, we get a client that uses software that is designed for personal finance for their business, and I strongly urge you not to use these software packages—especially if you are also using it for your personal accounts. While they are great solutions for personal finance, they do a poor job of providing reports for a business and separating the entity and personal data.

- **Specialized accounting software**—there are a wide variety of software packages that offer specialized solutions for specific industries as well as segments of your accounting systems. Just be careful in selecting these packages as sometimes they can create unnecessary complications that outweigh any benefits.

THE $200 ACCOUNTING SOLUTION MYTH

Thanks to very clever marketing by the large companies that sell the top accounting software packages, many new small business owners have bought into the myth that a $200 software package will instantly solve all their bookkeeping needs. Unfortunately, in the real world, there is much more involved in setting up an efficient accounting system that is customized to your business, supplies you with the reports you need to make informed decisions, and simplifies tax reporting.

QuickBooks and Peachtree are specifically designed for the small business owner with little or no accounting experience, and they now feature fixed asset and loan managers and improved chart of accounts templates. While it is fairly easy to set up a company file and start customizing the file to meet your business needs, a couple hours with a professional is an important investment that can save you countless hours of data entry and thousands of dollars in tax preparation fees. Plus, they will be able to tailor the reports to your business needs so that you can quickly get the information you need. Your CPA or tax professional would be the best person to set up and customize your accounting software file; however, there are also many good contract bookkeepers and QuickBooks consultants out there that may be more cost-effective, but they still need to talk to your tax preparer so that the file is set up optimally around your specific tax situation.

**QuickBooks/Peachtree Setup Services
Your Professional Should Provide**

- Customization of your chart of accounts,

- setup of classes to track segments of your business (if needed),

- setup of procedures for entering accounts receivable and accounts payable transactions,

- training on bank and credit card reconciliations,

- setup of electronic downloading of transactions,

- setup of procedures for efficient tracking of inventory,

- assistance with designing procedures for reporting unique to your business or industry, and

- setup of customized reports to meet internal reporting needs.

STRATEGIES FOR EFFICIENT SETUP
OF ACCOUNTING SOFTWARE FILES

The professional setting up your accounting software file should know your situation and have the best insight on the strategies that should be employed; however, the following are general strategies that apply to most small businesses and can save you time while also providing you with more effective reports. Most of the strategies are geared toward QuickBooks, but you could adapt them to Peachtree.

Using Classes to Track Segments or Separate Businesses

Classes are probably one of the easiest features to set up for a QuickBooks file, yet they are one of the most powerful features if used correctly. Basically, by adding an extra input field to each transaction and a small amount of additional data entry work, you will be able to quickly generate profit and loss reports for any segment, location, or other identifiable division in your business. If your company has several different businesses reported in one corporate entity, classes are a great alternative to creating separate QuickBooks files for each business. For medical practices with a large number of owners, classes are also a very effective option for tracking draws, expenses, and other transactions for each owner without cluttering your chart of accounts with long lists of sub-accounts.

Using Check Input Screens Instead of Entering and Paying Bills

For entering expenses and disbursements, QuickBooks allows you to enter bills when you receive them and then pay them at one time. This works well if you are on accrual basis and you have a large transaction volume; however, if your business reports on the cash basis method, you should only use bills and bill payments for vendors that have established a running balance with you. Otherwise, you are doubling your data entry and overcomplicating your accounting records. To pay an expense or disbursement, simply use the "Write Check" function and accomplish the same task in one step.

Only Create One Accumulated Depreciation Account

Some chart of account templates include separate accumulated depreciation accounts for each grouping of fixed assets, which does provide a more detailed balance sheet report. The problem is that this detail comes at a cost, as your tax professional has to complete additional reconciliation and more lengthy adjusting entries. Keep it simple for everyone and only create one accumulated depreciation account.

Use a Suspense Account for Your Tax Professional

QuickBooks actually has a default account called "Ask My Accountant" that was created for this very purpose. If you are entering transactions and do not know how to classify something, it is much more efficient for everyone if you post it to an account that your tax professional is guaranteed to review instead of just taking your best guess.

Maintaining Organized and Accurate Books

Now that you have your accounting system setup, the real challenge begins as it takes a lot of work to keep your books organized and accurate. The hard part is keeping current and making it a daily routine, but there are also several important practical steps you can take to make sure that your books will provide accurate reports.

- **Reconcile bank and credit card accounts monthly**—this is an essential task that has to be completed to find input errors, missing transactions, and stale checks needing to be voided. Accounting software greatly simplifies this process.

- **Review expense accounts monthly**—scan the expense account detail each month and look for transactions needing to be reclassified. Concentrate on critical accounts for your business as well as wages, payroll tax, and tax and licenses.

- **Adjust wage accounts monthly or quarterly to match reported amounts**—regardless of how you have your payroll processed, make sure your wage account(s) match the gross reported amounts. If they do not, make the needed adjustments so that they match.

- **Review balance sheet account detail monthly**—in addition to reviewing the expense accounts, you need to review the balance sheet account detail each month and adjust accounts as needed. Your tax professional should be reconciling these accounts when preparing the tax return, so if you need help with this task, they can point you in the right direction.

- **Reconcile fixed asset accounts and organize backup documentation**—review the account detail reports for your fixed asset accounts on a regular basis to make sure only capital expenditures are being posted to the accounts. Also, keep receipts and other documentation on file for all purchases recorded in the fixed asset accounts, and ask your tax professional to help with the journal entries for depreciation and fixed asset sales, trades, or dispositions.

- **Reconcile loan accounts and maintain amortization schedules**—review all current and long-term loan accounts to make sure only the principal portions of the payments are being posted to the loan accounts. Also, keep an updated amortization schedule for each loan owed by the business, and ask your tax professional for help with setting up any new loans or recording early payoffs.

What Your Tax Professional Should Provide

Unless you have a CPA or an experienced accountant on staff, your tax professional likely has to prepare a number of adjusting journal entries to make the corrections and reclassifications necessary for tax reporting purposes. In some cases, they may input as many as thirty entries, so it is crucial that they provide you with the adjusting journal entries necessary to update your accounting records. This is basic service that they should provide, and if you have QuickBooks, they can even send you a file that can automatically import their entries into your file.

If your tax professional is not providing you with adjusting journal entries each year, discuss it with them and find out why the entries are not being provided. If too many years pass without adjusting your QuickBooks file, you could be setting yourself up for problems if you later change accountants, as your new accountant will have to spend a lot of time reconciling your accounting records to the prior tax return. Also, make sure you receive depreciation schedules from your tax professional each year, as they are very important documents to have in your records.

PART II
Business Structure

Chapter 8

CHOOSING YOUR FORM OF BUSINESS

Selecting a form of business that is right for you and fits your needs is very difficult—especially if there are other owners and/or investors involved. There is a wide range of considerations that need to be addressed in the decision-making process including personal liability, taxes, state issues, and many other factors that will be discussed in this chapter. However, before you start to tense up, take a deep breath and relax for a bit as this is not necessarily a one-time decision that you will be stuck with for the life of your business. Most entities are fairly flexible, and there are opportunities for change along the way, but there are also some traps that you need to be aware of that can limit your options.

If you already have a business entity setup, it is always good to review your options as you should make sure you are re-evaluating your business structure from time to time to make sure it meets your short and long-term needs. Tax rules are constantly changing, IRS audit focus is always shifting, and new court cases come out each year that can change the tax strategies on which you may have based your entity selection and business structure. Whatever your situation, this chapter is a good source of information with which you can re-evaluate your business structure.

This chapter contains a brief overview of the different considerations that should be made when deciding on how to structure your business, as well as detailed information on each of the common business structure options available.

BUSINESS STRUCTURE CONSIDERATIONS

Deciding on how to structure your business requires careful evaluation of many different factors. While every business is different, below are some of the most important factors that need to be considered before deciding on how to structure your business.

- **Personal liability**—How much personal exposure do you have if there was a lawsuit brought against your business? Would your personal assets be at risk? How much additional protection could be gained from forming an entity, as compared to buying good liability insurance for a sole proprietorship? These are all issues that need to be discussed with your lawyer.

- **Number of owners/nature of relationship**— This is a huge factor to consider as it not only limits your choices, but it also complicates how the business will operate and keep equalization between owners. Also, some entities like the S corporation place restrictions on who can be owners.

- **Level of activity**—If your business has a low level of activity, you may not need the complication and cost of a corporation or LLC. On the other hand, if you are expecting large growth in your business, it may be worth setting up an entity that will still meet your needs in five years.

- **Profitability**—What does your expected profitability look like for the first five years? This is an important question to examine as losses in a C corporation carry forward and do not pass-through to the owner(s) like an S corporation or LLC.

- **Amount and Type of Debt**—What type of debt (if any) will your business have? An S corporation with losses and debt not in the shareholder's name can result in suspended losses due to lack of basis, whereas an LLC generally produces better results. Make sure you discuss this with your tax professional before deciding on an entity.

- **Fringe Benefits**—With health insurance costs rising so quickly, you may want to give extra consideration to the C corporation, which allows shareholders to take advantage of valuable fringe benefits. Given the right circumstances, this can be a big tax advantage.

- **State issues**—Some states, like Oregon and California, have minimum taxes for certain entity types that are assessed based on gross receipts, which can create large tax disadvantages. Also, if you will have owners working in different states, you may want to consider the personal income tax impact when deciding on how and where to organize set up your business.

- **Exit Strategy**—What does your exit strategy look like? Some go into business planning to sell within five years or as soon as it becomes marketable, while others plan on keeping the business long-term. Regardless of your current situation, you should discuss the exit strategy options with your lawyer and tax professional before deciding on an entity.

Business Structure Options

In order to make the best decision on how to structure your business, you need to have a general understanding of all the options available. The following overview will provide you with general information on each business entity, advantages and disadvantages, important tax issues, and warnings on tax traps that you need to be aware of. Detailed information on tax issues for the most popular entities—the S corporation and the limited liability company—can be found in the following two chapters.

Sole Proprietorships

The strange name should give it away; a sole proprietorship is the oldest form of business. It is also the most common and simplest form of business organization. Essentially, a sole proprietorship is an unincorporated business entity owned entirely by one individual. There can be no other owners; however, the IRS does allow husband and wife owned and operated businesses to be reported as a sole proprietorship.

Advantages

A sole proprietorship can be organized very informally as most states and local governments do not require much formal registration unless you want a "doing business as" (DBA) trade name to use for your business. Tax filing is simplified as the business income and deductions from a sole proprietorship are reported in the owner's 1040 tax return on Schedule C. The bookkeeping requirements are also much more relaxed since the IRS does not require sole proprietorships to report a balance sheet. This is especially true for sole proprietorships with a low volume of transactions, as they can typically get away with very simplified, non-computerized accounting records.

Disadvantages

The sole proprietorship is not a legally separate entity, so personal liability is a major concern for the owner and one of the biggest disadvantages of this simplified form of business organization. Some of that liability risk can be minimized with insurance, but even then, the risk of losing personal assets from litigation usually drives most owners to a limited liability company or a corporation. Another disadvantage is that the audit rates are much higher for businesses reported on Schedule C, which is understandable since the form is often self-prepared by taxpayers as compared with other entity returns that are too complicated to be prepared by taxpayers. Lastly, the tax on sole proprietors is a definite disadvantage as the entire amount of net income is subject to self-employment tax, whereas S corporations and LLCs have methods available to limit the amount of net income subject to the tax.

Partnerships

If you decide to go into business with others, the sole proprietorship is no longer an option (unless your only business partner is your spouse) and a vehicle is needed to split profit and loss, hold property, and share debt through. Of the business entities that fit the bill, the partnership is the most straightforward to set up. In fact, little if more than a handshake is needed to be recognized as a partnership by the IRS. However, even though partnerships offer ease of formation, partnership tax rules are some of the most complex in the Code, so it is critical to engage a tax professional to help you with the tax returns.

General vs. Limited Partnerships

There are two basic types of partnerships: general and limited partnerships. General partnerships are very similar to the sole proprietorship in that each owner is personally liable for all the debts and liabilities of the business and creditors can go after each partner's personal assets. In limited partnerships, only the general partners are personally liable for the business debts, and the limited partners are only liable up to their investment in the business. However, most small businesses are organized as general partnerships. Limited partnerships are mostly used in real estate investing, investment firms, and other groups of passive investors.

Partnership Tax Issues

For federal tax purposes, the partnership is a pass-through entity and does not pay any federal tax. Income and deductions reported on the Form 1065 return are allocated to each of the partners and reported on a Schedule K-1. Each partner then reports the pass through income and deduction items from the K-1 on their personal 1040 tax return. Form 1065 is much more complex than the Schedule C for sole proprietorships as the 1065 requires the reporting of the balance sheet of the business. Due to this complexity, I would strongly recommend against self-preparing Form 1065—even if you feel you have some accounting background. There are just too many chances for errors, and since it affects each partner's personal tax returns, it is always best to have an independent preparer.

General partnerships are often popular in states with high annual fees for LLCs and other business entities. For example, the great state of California charges a steep annual fee of $800 for even the smallest LLC. Then if your business has gross receipts over $250k, another $900 is due, so the general partnership has undoubtedly become very popular there despite the risk of personal liability. However, north of the border in Oregon, the minimum fee is much lower at $150, so general partnerships are a much less popular choice among new businesses.

Other Partnership-Based Entities

In addition to general partnerships, there are many partnership-based entities that share the same tax classification and are reported on Form 1065. The Limited Liability Company

(LLC) is the most popular partnership-based entity and will be discussed next, but most states also allow Limited Liability Partnerships (LLP), which are essentially LLCs designed for professionals and offer protection to partners for the misconduct and negligence of another partner.

Liability Company (LLC)

Chances are you probably already know a fair amount about the LLC, as it is likely the most popular entity of choice for new businesses after the S corporation. After all, who wouldn't want the liability protections of the corporation coupled with the ease of formation and flexibility of the partnership? It is a great combination, and as long as your state does not tax the LLC to death, it is a great form of organization for most small businesses that do not want the complexities that come with corporations.

LLC Tax Issues

Limited Liability Companies are pass-through entities like the general partnership and do not pay any federal tax at the LLC level. Instead, the owners of the LLC, called *members*, pay tax on their share of income and deductions passed through to them from the LLC. Like the general partnership, the income, deduction, and balance sheet information for the entity is reported on Form 1065, and members receive their share of income, deductions, and credits on Schedule K-1.

Even though the LLC is similar to the general partnership for tax purposes, there are some unique tax issues that LLC members need to understand with regards to self-employment tax and basis, which are covered in chapter 10.

Advantages of an LLC

One of the big advantages of the LLC, as compared to the S corporation, is that the LLC may distribute profits and losses disproportionately to its members using special allocations.

> ### Planning Tip
>
> LLCs have become especially popular for holding rental real estate and commercial buildings. This is due to the fact that appreciable property can be contributed to or distributed from an LLC without a taxable event. This provides important flexibility that corporations cannot offer, as distributions of appreciable property from corporations result in taxable gains.

This does require some special wording in your operating agreement, but it provides great flexibility in dealing with unique ownership situations and minority ownership.

Of course, the most important benefit is the limited liability for the members. Unlike general partnerships, creditors cannot come after the owners' personal assets. Liability is essentially limited to the investments of each member in the business—even for active members. In most states, this benefit makes for the best deal on insurance that you can buy. Just make sure you meet with an experienced lawyer and have them explain this in more detail before they complete your operating agreement—especially if you are setting up a multi-member LLC. Every business has unique circumstances, and a good small business lawyer will walk through all the scenarios and "what-ifs" that most small business owners often do not even consider.

Single Member Limited Liability Company (SMLLC)

While limited liability companies with one owner still enjoy the benefits of limited liability, there are some unfortunate tax consequences of not having other members. Even though the SMLLC is a legal entity, it is treated as a disregarded entity by the IRS, which means they see it as a "tax nothing" and do not have a special form for the entity to complete.

The IRS treats SMLLCs the same as a sole proprietorship and requires them to report income and deductions on Schedule C in the owner's personal 1040 tax return. The worst part of this treatment is that all net income is subject to self-employment tax. The simple fact that a SMLLC only has one member unfortunately restricts the owner from using tax strategies available to multiple member LLCs that would minimize the net income subject to self-employment tax.

To get around this tax disadvantage, there are some solutions. For married taxpayers, simply make your spouse an owner in the LLC. Even if you only give them 1 percent in the entity, it solves the problem and gives you better tax treatment. If you are single, consider electing to be taxed as a corporation for federal tax purposes and then elect S corporation status. This strategy lets you remain an LLC for legal purposes, which makes it easier to manage, but also gives you the preferential tax treatment available to S corporations.

Corporation (C Corporation)

By far, the most complex and expensive way of doing business is the corporation. The legal costs alone to set up and maintain a corporation are enough to easily eclipse the costs of an LLC, partnership, or sole proprietorship, but then you have additional accounting fees, incorporation charges, annual fees, and sometimes state minimum income taxes based on gross receipts or capital. It makes sense if you think of big corporations like Apple, GM, or AT&T® and realize that many of the same basic corporate rules and documentation formalities apply to small corporations as well.

There are two types of corporations in the eyes of the tax code: *C* and *S* corporations (the letters refer to the related subchapters of the tax code). All corporations start as C corporations initially, and then for those corporations wanting to be S corporations, an S election is filed with the IRS, which we discuss further in chapter 9. This section focuses on C corporations and examines the benefits and disadvantages of the entity.

Fringe Benefits

Despite the costs and complexities of forming and maintaining a corporation, there are important benefits and advantages to the corporation. One the most important benefits, especially in light of rising health care costs, are the fringe benefits available to C corporation shareholders and not to owners of other entities. In a corporation, shareholders are treated like regular employees and can take advantage of health fringe benefits like a medical reimbursement plan or disability insurance. This is an important advantage over more than 2 percent S corporation shareholders, who are excluded from participating in employee fringe benefits. LLC members, partners in partnerships, and sole proprietors are also excluded from employee fringe benefits as they are self-employed. Given the right circumstances and high medical costs, the C corporation can result in big tax savings for shareholders; however, you have to have your tax professional run the numbers carefully and consider all other factors as the true net savings may not be as substantial.

Temporary Tax Benefits

In addition to fringe benefits, many new business owners have been lured to the corporation over the last few years because of the low 15 percent dividend tax rate and temporary incentives that offered gain exclusions on small business stock sales. In fact, some short cycle businesses that planned to run five years and then sell likely benefited from these rules; however, I would recommend some caution for new small business owners as the 15 percent dividend rate will likely not be extended beyond 2012 and gain on stock sale exclusions are very limited as you could end up having to sell assets rather than stock.

Corporation Tax Issues

The C corporation pays tax based on net income at special corporate tax rates (see the Federal Corporate Tax Rates table below). While, the first $50,000 of net income is only taxed at

15 percent, the tax quickly goes up from there, so most C corporation owners try to pay themselves enough in wages to keep net income below $50,000. In addition to the tax at corporate level, if the taxed profits are later distributed to the shareholders as dividends, theoretically there is a "double tax" at the individual level on the dividends. However, in reality, there rarely ends up being an actual double tax for small businesses since most if not all of a C corporation's earnings are usually paid out in wages to the shareholder employee(s).

Federal Corporate Income Tax Rates		
Taxable income over	Not over	Tax rate
$ - $	50,000	15%
50,000	75,000	25%
75,000	100,000	34%
100,000	335,000	39%
335,000	10,000,000	34%
10,000,000	15,000,000	35%
15,000,000	18,333,333	38%
18,333,333	. . . .	35%

The Built-in Gains Tax

Most business owners view the C corporation tax issues as disadvantageous as compared to the S corporation, and if the IRS did not have such a big tax penalty in place to keep existing C corporations from electing S status, there would likely be very few small business C corporations remaining today. That penalty is a very complex tax called the built-in gains tax (or "BIG" tax), which requires extensive calculations, valuations, and long-term planning.

The BIG tax requires a C corporation to measure the amount of unrecognized appreciation in the corporation at time of S election, which requires determining the fair market value of assets and comparing them to the corporation's tax basis in the assets. The built-in gains or losses on the assets are then netted and you end up with a net unrecognized built-in gain. From that point, depending on your circumstances, you may have a large tax due in the year of the

S election, or you may be able to avoid the tax by incurring net losses in each of the ten years of the recognition window.

If you have a C corporation and would like explore the idea of electing S status, take the time to sit down with your tax professional and find out what the BIG tax would look like for your corporation. They will have to perform some in-depth analysis and make calculations for the different options available, but it is usually money well spent even if the result is that it would be too costly to elect S status. If your corporation is on the cash basis, be prepared for some bad news before even getting to any calculations or analysis, as the unrecognized gains on accounts receivable often makes the S election far too costly.

S Corporation

The S corporation is the most popular entity of choice among new business owners, with the exception of the sole proprietorship, and it usually only takes a few years of paying self-employment tax before most profitable sole proprietors jump to the S corporation. This is due to the fact that the S corporation provides a strategy for minimizing employee and employer payroll taxes for the shareholder (the corporate equivalent of self-employment tax) by paying a reasonable

---

Warning!

Do not purchase commercial buildings, rental real estate, or any other type of appreciable real property within a C or S corporation. Do not contribute this type of property to a corporation either. The tax ramifications on a later distribution of property are very negative within a corporation as it creates a taxable event. If you have a commercial building in a corporation that was purchased thirty years ago before the LLC option was available, it is a little more understandable; however, now there is no reason to make this mistake.

---

wage to shareholders. The S corporation is also a pass-through entity like the partnership and LLC, so many of the concerns that business owners have about C corporations, like the "double-tax", are no longer an issue.

Despite the tax advantages of the S corporation, there are many rules and complexities that S corporation shareholders need to understand, and a brief overview would not do them justice, so chapter 9 provides detailed information on the S election, reasonable compensation, distributions, shareholder loans, and basis.

Qualified Personal Service Corporation (QPSC)

New qualified personal service corporations are quite rare these days, and that is due to the fact that QPSCs became popular back when corporations were necessary to qualify for tax-deferred retirement plans. Since that time, employee benefit laws have been expanded to create parity between corporate shareholders and the self-employed, and LLCs and LLPs are now available to professionals in most states. For those of you who are still structured as a QPSC, it is likely due to the fact that it would be too costly to dissolve and form a new entity. There is nothing wrong with this strategy, and in many cases it works very well as tax savings from moving to an S corporation or LLC/LLP would be very minimal.

The annual routine with a QPSC requires a lot of pre-planning on your tax professional's part as wages have to paid-out before the tax year-end so that there is no taxable income. Otherwise, a flat rate of 35 percent applies to the taxable income. There are other complications for your tax professional, so make sure you have a good tax professional with a lot of experience with QPSCs.

Chapter 9

S Corporation Tax Issues

Over the past fifteen years, the number of S corporations has quadrupled. With the exception of sole proprietorships, S corporations are the most popular form of small business in the United States. This should come as no surprise given the self-employment tax savings the structure provides, and even though the S corporation is a solid entity choice, there are many tax considerations that a small business owner should be aware of. The tax savings from forming an S corporation can easily be erased by an IRS audit if you are not operating your S corporation correctly, and claiming ignorance is not going to get you anywhere.

This chapter will cover the S election, reasonable compensation, distributions, shareholder loans, basis, shareholder health insurance, and late filing penalties. This information is vital for anyone with an S corporation or considering electing S corporation status.

S Corporation Basics

For tax purposes, an S corporation is most commonly a corporation that elects S status. However, it can also be a non-corporate entity, like an LLC, that elects to be taxed as a corporation and then elects S status. The latter type of S corporation is becoming more popular as it combines the legal flexibility of non-corporate entities with the preferential tax treatment of the S corporation.

Generally, S corporations are not subject to income taxes at the corporation level. In fact, they are often referred to as "pass-through" entities as income, deductions, losses, and credits are passed through to the corporation's shareholders, based on each shareholder's percentage of stock ownership. In many ways, S corporations closely parallel the taxation of partnerships, and many of the rules that apply to partners of partnerships also apply to shareholders of S corporations. However, corporations electing S status are governed by the same corporate tax rules applicable to C corporations— especially with regard to matters like capital contributions, redemptions, and liquidations.

Who May Elect S Corporation Status?

Electing S corporation status is no longer limited to eligible corporations. Thanks to "check the box" regulations, eligible entities electing to be taxed as corporations for federal tax purposes can elect S corporation status as well. These eligible entities would include LLCs and partnerships that filed Form 8832.

To be considered an eligible for S corporation election, the following requirements must be met:

- The entity must be a domestic corporation or eligible entity electing to be taxed as a corporation. This means the entity must be organized under the laws of any state or U.S. territory.

- Shareholders can only be individuals, estates, certain trusts, banks, and certain exempt organizations. Partnerships and corporations cannot be shareholders (although SMLLCs can). No foreign trusts and traditional or Roth IRAs.

- Only citizens or residents of the United States can be shareholders.

- The corporation can have only one class of stock.

In addition, an S corporation can have no more than 100 shareholders. For purposes of applying this limit, a husband and wife are counted as a single shareholder, and in many cases, all qualifying members of a family who hold corporation stock are also treated as a single shareholder. However, rarely is this limit a problem for small businesses.

How Is the S Corporation Status Elected?

For eligible corporations and entities, the election to be treated as an S corporation is made by filing Form 2553, which is a crucial document that should be completed by a lawyer or tax professional and sent by certified mail.

To be effective for the current year, Form 2553 must be filed on or before the fifteenth day of the third month of that year. Elections made after that date are deemed effective for the following year. However, the IRS does provide automatic relief for late elections in some cases.

Relief for Late S Elections

There are three revenue procedures (Rev. Proc. 2007-62, 2004-48, and 2003-43) that have been released to provide relief for late elections, and each has different timelines and rather complex requirements, so talk to your tax professional about it and they can let you know if you qualify. Given the right circumstances, you can even file the election within twenty-four months of the original due date.

If you discover that an S election was never made and twenty-four months or more have passed since the original due date of the election, or you do not meet the requirements for any of these revenue procedures, you will likely have to wait a year to become an S corporation. In addition, any S corporation returns that have already been filed with the IRS must be amended, which can dramatically change your tax liability and result in penalties and interest. You can try pleading with the IRS to allow the late election; however, your chances of success will be very poor. I have only witnessed one example in over ten years in public accounting where the IRS accepted an S election that was over twenty-four months late as a result of outright pleading; but it was a very messy situation where a large amount of trust fund payroll taxes were owed, and I think the IRS did not want to deal with all the amended returns that would have resulted if they disallowed the S election. Other than pleading with the IRS, your only other option is to request a private letter ruling, which is a very expensive process that I would not recommend.

Important!

When you receive your S corporation acceptance letter from the IRS, make sure you keep the document in your permanent file, as it is an extremely important proof of your election. When taking on new S corporation clients, I try to always ask for a copy as I have witnessed far too many ugly surprises with new clients that claimed to have filed the S election.

THE MOST POPULAR TAX BENEFIT
OF THE S CORPORATION

As discussed in chapter 8, the main tax advantage of the S corporation is the ability to minimize self-employment taxes that sole proprietorships, partnerships and LLCs are

---

Example

Mike is the sole shareholder of an S corporation and takes an annual wage of $55,000. For 2012, his net taxable income from the S corporation is $45,000 and he took cash distributions of $40,000. Mike pays employee and employer taxes and personal income tax on the $55,000 and then only pays personal income tax on the $45,000 of net income. Had he been a sole proprietorship, he would not have paid himself a wage, and the net taxable income would be $100,000, which would all be subject to self-employment tax and personal income tax. Therefore, the tax savings in this simplified example would be the self-employment taxes that would have been paid on the $45,000 of net income.

---

subject to, while avoiding the potential for double-taxation that a C corporation could have. Ordinary income that passes through from the S corporation to the shareholder is only subject to income tax and not self-employment tax. This special tax treatment is only available because the S corporation is required to pay "reasonable compensation" to the shareholders and the employee and employer payroll tax on that compensation is roughly the equivalent of self-employment tax. The resulting tax savings is the difference between the payroll taxes paid on the reasonable compensation and the self-employment tax that would have been paid on the wages and the net taxable income.

What Is Reasonable Compensation?

A reasonable wage needs to be paid to shareholders that own more than a 2 percent interest in an S corporation, but what is reasonable and who decides it? This is a crucial question to examine as an S corporation shareholder. After all, if this reasonable wage number is going to have such a dramatic effect on your tax savings, you need to understand how to determine the wage in a way that will not cause problems down the road and possibly unravel your entire tax strategy.

To explain reasonable compensation, let's look at what is clearly not reasonable. Paying zero or nominal amounts for wages is definitely unreasonable in most cases, especially if you took cash distributions from the S corporation. Almost all court cases on unreasonable compensation have ruled that paying zero wages is unreasonably low compensation. The only valid exception would likely be an S corporation that is losing money and the shareholder is contributing money and not taking any distributions. Other than that scenario, S corporations need to pay reasonable wages to their more than 2 percent shareholders if they want to avoid the attention of the IRS. This has become more urgent in recent years as the IRS rolled out the Inadequate Compensation Project that specifically addresses this issue, so make sure to steer clear of the obvious red flag of zero wages.

In concept, a reasonable compensation amount is essentially based on what is typically paid to comparable employees in the industry or what would be paid to an employee to do the work performed by the shareholder. To determine this reasonable wage amount, you have to look at the employee's role in the company and their qualifications, as well as the size and type of company. In audits, IRS agents always seem to use wage data from Salary.com or a similar site; however, determining a reasonable wage is much more complex than that as you have to apply the specific characteristics of the company and the employee to any external comparison data from websites. Additionally, you have to consider what you would have to pay to hire someone to do your job. For example, if you sold your business to an investor who did not want to run or manage the day-to-day operations, they would have to hire a manager to run the business, so you will want to estimate the wage amount that would have to be paid to this hypothetical manager and factor it into your decision on reasonable compensation.

Who Determines the Reasonable Compensation Amount?

Ideally, a shareholder should perform an analysis each year to make sure their wage remains reasonable, but too many S corporation owners continue to pay the same wage amount that was decided upon with their CPA back when they incorporated. Even worse, some S corporation owners do not even understand the basics behind the reasonable wage and were simply sold a tax savings package by their tax professional in order save on self-employment tax. You need to understand that the responsibility to select a reasonable wage ultimately lies with you. If the S corporation tax concepts are confusing to you, make sure you have your tax professional explain it more detail. If you are like me and learn better with visuals, have them lay out the numbers in a way that allows you to see the impact of the reasonable wage in terms of actual tax dollars. The bottom line is that you need to understand the impact of your decision in selecting a wage as the IRS has authority to reclassify distributions as wages in audit if they find that your wages are not reasonable.

Red Flag Warning

If you have a one-shareholder S corporation, the IRS can quickly analyze your wages by comparing two lines on Form 1120S—Officer Compensation on line 7 in the deductions section of the first page and Distributions on line 7 of Schedule M-2 on page 4. This shows them the amount of the reasonable wage paid to the shareholder compared to the amount of cash distributions taken over and above that wage, and while it is not an indicator of whether the wage is actually reasonable, it can be a red flag indicator if the numbers are widely out of proportion. For example, if you are a doctor who only takes a wage of $40,000 but your distributions are $260,000, your proportion of wages to distributions could definitely draw the attention of the IRS.

Recent IRS Audit Developments
There have been recent reports among tax professionals that the IRS has stepped up reasonable compensation audits on S corporations and is requesting extremely detailed information and documents. Such audits can be very costly as they not only hit you with employer and employee taxes, but they also assess sizable penalties. While you should have a healthy fear of these audits, you should not be so scared that you think you need to raise your wage above a reasonable amount just to be safe. The law only requires your wage be reasonable, and often in audits the IRS goes too far by arguing that your wage is not reasonable enough, but as long as you have strong factual support for your wage, you should be able to find success against the IRS on the this issue if you have a good tax professional or lawyer representing you.

WHAT ARE DISTRIBUTIONS?

A common area of confusion for S corporation owners is distributions, which are withdrawals of earnings by a shareholder over and above their reasonable salary. Also referred to as draws or dividends, distributions can be taken at any time or not at all. Some shareholders take all their earnings, even amounts in excess of earnings, while others only take minimal distributions in order to retain cash in the corporation. S corporation shareholders are not taxed based on the amount of distributions as they are just withdrawals of earnings; however, there can be cases in which excess distributions not converted to loans to shareholder can result in capital gains.

Distributions Must Be Proportionate to Ownership
One unique requirement of S corporation distributions is that they must be made in proportion to ownership. In other words, if there are two shareholders owning 60 percent and

---

Tip for family-owned S corporations

If all the shareholders of your S corporation are family members and you are having a hard time keeping distributions proportionate, you can use gifting to even out any differences and avoid having to create loan to shareholder accounts. Your tax professional can help you with this, but it is an important strategy to use if there are a lot of personal transactions causing disproportionate distributions.

---

40 percent of an S corporation, a total distribution of $10,000 must be paid as individual distributions of $6,000 and $4,000 respectively. Obviously, this is not a problem for single owner S corporations, but it can cause problems for all other S corporations—especially if there are minority owners.

If this is the first time you have heard about this rule, it is likely because your tax professional is making adjustments to make distributions proportionate, which often includes reclassifying amounts to shareholder loan accounts. Make sure you have your tax professional explains any of these adjustments so that you understand the tax impact. Years of accumulated adjustments to make distributions proportionate can end up haunting you years later with undesirable tax consequences.

Personal Transactions Paid by the Corporation

In a perfect world, paying proportionate distributions would not be a problem; however, corporations often pay for personal expenses as a convenience for the shareholder, and rarely are these personal transactions ever proportionate. These personal expenses often include personal items from combined purchases, expenses for another business entity owned by a shareholder, life or disability insurance premiums, the personal portion of travel expenses, and any other nondeductible expenses that are not proportionate to ownership.

There is nothing wrong with the corporation paying personal expenses for a shareholder as long as you have good documentation and there is proper classification in the accounting records so that the expenses are not deducted. The only problem is that typically one shareholder has a larger amount of personal expenses paid by the corporation, so either some equalizing is necessary or the personal expenses have to go against a shareholder loan account. Another solution is that the shareholder with the larger personal expenses can just reimburse the corporation for the difference, or the shareholders can simply pay for these items personally, which is an easy way to eliminate this problem altogether.

WHAT ARE SHAREHOLDER LOANS?

An S corporation is a separate legal entity from the shareholder, and therefore any transactions between the corporation and shareholder have to be formally documented as wages, distributions, loans, stock purchases and sales, or reimbursements. A shareholder loan is often the result of:

- funds contributed to the company to be paid back in the future,

- the payment of business expenses by the shareholder personally,

- reclassified personal expenses or excess distributions, and

- the use of personal credit cards or loans for the business.

S corporation shareholders cannot have an open, undocumented account for all personal transactions, as this can be seen as a separate class of stock. In severe cases, this can cause the corporation to lose its S election since one of the four requirements of an S corporation is that it only has one class of stock. Loans have to be documented and can either be loans to or loans from the shareholder depending on the balance at any point in time.

Shareholder Loan Documentation

If you were to loan me $20,000 today, would you insist on loan documents, regular payments, and interest? Of course you would! Such requirements and documentation would seem to be common sense, so why do many shareholders fail treat the loans to their S corporations the same way?

In my experience with S corporations over the years, lack of shareholder loan documentation is common in single-owner and family-owned S corporations and is often the result of owners getting behind on the accounting records and lack of understanding of how certain shareholder trans-actions should be handled. It is also common among smaller S corporations that try to minimize their legal costs or go the do-it-yourself route, as an attorney that is being fully engaged would prepare documentation to support any new share-holder loans.

Regardless of your situation, completing documentation is very important if you want to avoid problems with the IRS in the event of an audit. The following are basic steps you can take to make sure your documentation will keep you out of trouble:

- If you loan funds to the S-Corporation, prepare a demand note to document the loan. If possible, try to have the corporation make regularly scheduled repayments or accrue interest.

- Keep personal expenditures paid by the corporation to a minimum.

- If you pay for business expenses personally, have the corporation reimburse you rather than increasing the loan from shareholder.

- Try to use one credit card exclusively for the business and one for personal expenditures, as it reduces the shareholder transactions that you have to document.

- If you take a loan from the corporation or have excess distributions classified as a loan to shareholder, make sure to accrue interest on balances over $10,000.

Loans from Shareholder

Upon incorporation, S corporation shareholders often loan funds to the corporation after paying for the stock and contributing fixed assets. Larger loans are set up formally with interest and payment terms, while some small loans are just short-term loans to cover the start-up cash flow needs. Throughout the life of the S corporation they may loan additional funds as needed, receive repayments from the corporation, or reclassify personal expenses paid by the corporation and excess distributions against the loan. If there are some large reclassifications of excess distributions and personal expenses, a loan from shareholder can change to a loan to shareholder.

Loans to Shareholder

It may seem a little strange that a shareholder would actually owe money to their S corporation, but such a scenario is actually quite common. Loans from an S corporation to a shareholder are usually not initiated by the shareholder like a normal loan. In fact, some shareholders are likely unaware they owe funds to their own corporation. This is because most loans to the shareholder are the result of excess distributions or personal expenses that created disproportionate distributions, which had to be adjusted by their tax professional. While most tax professionals try to explain these adjustments sufficiently when the decision is made to convert the excess distributions to a loan, part of the problem is that it is often seen as a temporary issue that will work itself out the next year, and so small business owners often forget about the balance. Unfortunately, if there is insufficient income to clear the loan the next year, or if the shareholder again took excess distributions, the balance will grow. Once the balance grows to over $10k, you should start accruing interest on the loan.

Ongoing loans to an S corporation shareholder can cause problems for both the corporation and the shareholder. For the corporation, acquiring or maintaining bank loans or lines of credit may be difficult if the shareholder has large ongoing loans to shareholder. In the last few years the banks have dramatically tightened lending requirements for small businesses, and a material loan to shareholder is a red flag that can indicate that the shareholder is taking too much cash out of the business. For the shareholder, amounts owed to the corporation can result in additional tax upon sale or exit from the business, which can be a very unwelcome surprise.

Shareholder Basis: The Key to Deductible Losses

Shareholder basis is an area of tax law that you do not learn about as a small business owner unless you have ever had insufficient basis for your losses, and even then few of these owners understand much beyond their specific circumstances. At times, calculating and understanding basis can even be challenging for seasoned tax professionals, so while small business owners do not need an in-depth understanding of basis, they should understand the basics so that they are not caught off guard by suspended losses.

What Is Basis and How Is It Calculated?

Shareholder basis is, at its most basic level, the balance of a shareholder's investment in a corporation at a specific point in time. This balance has to be tracked because of the unique structure of the S corporation, and the fact that while income, deductions, non-deductible expenses, and distributions have to be allocated according to each shareholder's percentage of ownership, shareholders typically contribute different amounts to an S corporation because of shareholder loans. One shareholder may loan large amounts to an S corporation to help finance the business while other shareholders' only investment may be their stock purchase. Since the S corporation is a flow-through entity and items of income, deduction, and credits flow through to the shareholders personally, basis has to be tracked on the shareholder level to make sure any losses or deductions can be deducted on the shareholder's individual tax return.

Initial Basis upon Incorporation

The following is a simplified overview of the basis calculation so that you have a basic understanding of how it works. There are many complications and special rules, so make sure you have your tax professional walk you through your basis statement if your basis balance is different than expected.

In a new S corporation, a shareholder's initial basis would be the:

- cost of the stock purchased,
- amount of any loans to the corporation, and
- the lower of adjusted basis or fair market value of any property transferred to the corporation in exchange for stock.

This initial basis amount is fairly straightforward as it represents your overall investment in the S corporation, but it gets more complicated from this point.

Basis Calculation at Year-End

At the end of the first tax year, the initial basis amount would then be increased by:

- ordinary net business income,

- separately-stated items of income or gain, and new shareholder loans to the corporation.

After adding the above items, the basis balance is then reduced by:

- non-deductible expenses (like 50 percent of meals and entertainment),

- shareholder loan repayments,

- distributions of cash or the fair market value of property, and

- any net losses or separately-stated deductions.

This process is then repeated each tax year, so shareholder basis is essentially a running balance of your investment in the company. Once a shareholder's basis balance is depleted, losses generated by an S corporation are no longer deductible on the shareholder's individual tax return. Instead, these losses are considered suspended and carry forward until basis is restored.

To further complicate the calculation, there are ordering rules and the loan and stock basis balances are actually tracked separately. While much is this complication is for your tax professional to worry about, there is one ordering rule that small business owners should be aware of—especially if your S corporation has a large amount of meals and entertainment expenses each year. Basically, non-deductible expenses—like the non-deductible half of meals and entertainment expense—have to reduce basis before business losses. There is an election that can be made to claim deductible losses first, but most S corporations follow the standard rules. This rule is important as it can make a big difference when a shareholder has insufficient basis for a loss.

Example

Joe starts an S corporation for his plumbing business with two other shareholders in January 2012. He purchases stock with $10,000 cash and also loans $30,000 to the business. His initial basis is $40,000. Joe and his fellow shareholders have a hard time getting the revenue to flow, and at the end of the year he receives his K-1 with a loss of $39,000 and non-deductible expenses of $3,000. If Joe did not receive any distributions or loan repayments, his basis at the end of 2012 would be zero and he would have suspended losses of $2,000. The non-deductible expenses had to reduce basis first before the losses could be taken into consideration, which is why only $37,000 in losses could be deducted in 2012.

For the most part, the end result is that you basically get in losses and expenses what you put into the company. In other words, you cannot deduct a loss that was generated by expenses paid for with funds loaned from other shareholders or another source.

Debt That Does Not Provide Basis

What type of debt you have in an S corporation is critically important, as it is often the difference between a deductible loss and a suspended loss. Debt that is in the name of the corporation does not create basis for the shareholders. Even if the shareholders personally guarantee the loan, there is generally no basis given until the shareholder makes good on a guarantee by making actual payments. This would include credit cards, lines of credit, and other loans that are in the name of the S corporation, so make sure to discuss this with your tax professional before setting up financing for your business.

Any funds transferred to the corporation from personal loans or credit cards in the shareholder's name create basis for the shareholder. These amounts would basically be structured as loans from the shareholder. The only downside with the personal loans is that there is no limited liability protection with regards to the loan since it is outside the corporation.

Basis Reporting and Recordkeeping

Basis for each shareholder has to be reconciled and reported each year with the S corporation tax return, which is why preparation of the tax return should always be left to a competent tax professional. A shareholder's basis is reported on a schedule that accompanies the K-1 supplied to the shareholder, and if a shareholder is claiming deduction for their share of an aggregate loss, the basis schedule actually has to be submitted with their individual tax return. Even though tax professionals are responsible for calculating basis, ultimately it is the responsibility of the shareholder to prove basis to the IRS, so make sure you keep any basis information supplied to you.

Reporting Health Insurance

for Shareholders

The reporting of health insurance premiums for a more than 2 percent S corporation shareholder can be a little confusing; however, it is crucial that it is reported correctly if you want to maximize your deduction. If you miss a few simple steps before the end of the year, you could end up limiting or losing your deduction all together.

The self-employed health insurance deduction allows self-employed individuals to deduct their health insurance premiums on the front of the 1040 as an adjustment against income. Even though an S corporation shareholder is not technically self-employed, the IRS requires a more than 2 percent S corporation shareholder to report the deduction as if they were self-employed and not on the S corporation return.

Simple Steps to Maximize Your Deduction

Below are the steps that have to be taken in order to get the self-employed health insurance deduction. Make sure you follow them closely as an error can result in the loss of substantial tax savings.

- An S corporation cannot deduct health, dental, or other medical premiums for a shareholder who owns more than 2 percent. Their premiums should be tracked separately in the accounting system throughout the year.

- If the corporation did not pay the premiums during the year, make sure the corporation reimburses them before the end of the year.

- Before the final payroll run of the year, calculate the total shareholder health, dental, and other medical insurance premiums paid or reimbursed by the corporation as this figure will be needed for the final payroll and the shareholder's W-2.

- The amount of premiums for the year is paid to the shareholder as payroll, but there is special payroll tax treatment for this payment. The amount is subject to Federal and State withholding, but it is not subject to social security or Medicare tax. If you use a payroll service, they will have a pay item for this specific payment.

- On the W-2, the amount of the premiums is recorded in box 1 wages, in the state wages, and in box 14 as "S/H Health Ins" or a similar description.

- Finally, on the shareholder's individual tax return, make sure the amount of shareholder health insurance is deducted as self-employed health insurance on the front of Form 1040.

The end result is that the payroll payment for the premiums is deducted as a wage on the corporation return, the wage is taxed as income on the individual return, and the self-employed health insurance deduction is taken on the personal return, which all nets out to a deduction in the amount of the premiums. This may seem like a whole lot of unnecessary paperwork, but it is much better than the treatment that results if you do not follow these steps.

Tax Consequences of Incorrect Reporting

If a more than 2 percent shareholder fails to include their health insurance premiums on their W-2, technically the IRS will not allow the self-employed health insurance deduction on the individual return, and the shareholder would have to claim the premiums as a medical expense on Schedule A, which unfortunately is subject to a haircut of 7.5 percent of adjusted gross income (10 percent starting in 2013). This means that your deduction is reduced by an amount equal to 7.5 percent of your adjusted gross income, and if there is anything left then you get a deduction for the remaining amount. If you run the numbers, this is huge loss of deduction and a horrible penalty for not following the IRS rules.

Given the high cost of health insurance premiums these days, it is very important that you make sure and follow the steps listed above each year. Have your tax professional help you and do not wait until tax time as amended W-2s can be costly to prepare.

LATE FILING PENALTIES

Back in December 2007, the 110th Congress passed the Alternative Minimum Tax Relief Act of 2007, and buried in the small print of the bill was a revenue raiser that ended up unfairly penalizing S corporations for filing their tax returns late. Unfortunately, few knew about this new tax law until the penalty notices started arriving, and even today, many S corporation shareholders are being shocked by this penalty that can result in staggering fees.

S corporation tax returns are generally due March 15 following the calendar year-end. If an extension is filed by March 15, the deadline is extended six months and the final deadline becomes September 15. While some type of penalty for late filing is probably fair, the current penalty is not really fair since there is not an automatic abatement provision for smaller S corporations like the one available to entities that file a partnership tax return. Partnerships and LLCs have Revenue Procedure 84-35, which allows domestic entities who file a Form 1065 with ten or fewer partners to get automatic penalty relief. Unfortunately, a similar revenue procedure was never issued for S corporations.

The fee is currently $195 per shareholder *AND* $195 per month that the return is late. This means if you have two shareholders and your return was four months late, you have a whopping $1,560 fee! At six months late, you would be looking at $2,340! This should give you twenty-three hundred good reasons to make sure the return is timely filed or extended if it cannot be filed by March 15. This is not something you can take lightly anymore, and if a bookkeeper, owner, or tax professional is causing delays, the issue needs to be address and corrected immediately.

If this advice comes to you too late and you have received a penalty notice, there is some hope if you have good history of timely filing with the IRS. At least in the first year of the penalty, the IRS was giving one-time consideration based on a good history of timely filing and paying, so if this applies to you, write a letter requesting abatement and the IRS may grant your request. If you do not have good history or if it is your second late filing penalty, all you can fall back on is reasonable cause, which can be very difficult to successfully argue. If you are in this situation, contact your attorney or tax professional and have them argue the case for you.

Chapter 10

LIMITED LIABILITY COMPANY TAX ISSUES

While not as complicated as the S corporation, limited liability companies (LLCs) do have a number of tax issues that members need to be aware of and understand. Chief among them is the self-employment tax issue, which is just as crucial as the reasonable compensation issue for S corporations and central to the tax savings the LLC provides. This chapter will also cover member basis and late filing penalties.

This chapter only addresses tax issues for LLCs with multiple members. Single-member limited liability companies (SMLLCs) are not taxed as partnerships and are covered in chapter 8.

SELF-EMPLOYMENT TAX

Most business owners are looking to reduce self-employment tax, and often tax professionals promote the LLC as a vehicle to accomplish this while avoiding the complexities of the S corporation. After all, with the right circumstances, a multi-member LLC can save just as much tax as an S corporation. The only difference is that there is much more authoritative support for the S corporation reasonable wage strategy than the wide variety of self-employment tax strategies for the LLC.

With an S corporation, a reasonable wage is paid to the shareholder and the corporate equivalent of self-employment tax is paid on these wages while the remaining amount of distributive income is only subject to income tax (which we discuss in detail in chapter 9). With an LLC, most of the self-employment tax strategies center around a guaranteed payment, which is similar to a reasonable wage, that is paid to the member for services and subject to self-employment tax, while any other distributed income is treated as return on investment and not subject to self-employment tax. Despite the similarities to the S corporation strategies, the LLC strategies have much more variation and unfortunately have very little authoritative support, which is due to the fact that both the IRS and Congress have failed to address the issue ever since the IRS proposed regulations on the matter were shot down in 1997.

Proposed IRS Regulation
In January 1997, the IRS issued proposed regulations that specifically addressed the LLC self-employment tax issue and set out rules for determining when LLC members are subject to self-employment tax (Prop. Reg. §1.1402(a)-2(h)(2)). While the regulations may have had a good conceptual framework, they created a political firestorm as many politicians, including Newt Gingrich, saw it as a "stealth tax" since it was the result of an IRS regulation and not an Act of Congress. Congress ended up intervening and prohibited the IRS from making the proposed regulations final until July 1, 1998. The IRS ended up backing down on the issue, and since that time, the issue has not been revisited by Congress or the IRS. Whether it was the Lewinsky scandal that

distracted Congress or the US Embassy bombings, July 1998 came and went, and fourteen years later we still have no finalized regulations on the matter.

The point of this short history lesson was not to encourage you to reminisce, but to give you some background on the predicament that LLC members face in trying to find guidance on how to deal with self-employment tax. Without any final regulations or an Act of Congress, we are left with looking at the concepts behind the proposed regulations and then making our best attempt at forming reasonable strategies for determining self-employment income.

The Limited Partner

The Internal Revenue Code contained similar rules on self-employment tax for partnerships long before the 1997 IRS proposed regulations on LLCs. Basically, IRC §1402(a)(13) provides that when a taxpayer is a limited partner in a partnership, the taxpayer's distributive share of income or loss from that partnership is not subject to self-employment tax. How this rule was to be applied to LLCs and their members is what the proposed regulations attempted to answer.

According to the proposed regulations, an LLC member will not be treated as a limited partner for purposes of self-employment if the individual:

- has personal liability for the debts of the partnership,

- has authority to contract on behalf of the partnership, or

- participates in the partnership's business for more than 500 hours during the taxable year.

In addition to this general rule, the proposed regulations also contain complex rules that allow an LLC member who fails the general rule to qualify as a limited partner; however, they involve setting up separate classes of interest in an LLC, which will not work for everyone and can be costly. Overall, the proposed regulations make it difficult for most small business LLC members to qualify as limited partners for self-employment tax purposes, but remember that the regulations have not been finalized and have no legal effect until they become final. The concepts are the important part as they lay the foundation for many of the current strategies used by tax professionals.

Current Strategies
It is extremely difficult to develop strategies to minimize self-employment tax for LLC members when there is no authoritative guidance to follow. Most would agree that claiming none of your income as self-employment income is not a good idea, but claiming all of your distributive income as self-employment income is probably too conservative of an approach, so somewhere between all and none is a reasonable amount.

The Proposed Regulations Approach
The safe approach would be to follow the proposed regulations closely and work with your lawyer and tax professional to set up separate ownership interests in your LLC—one for general member interest and the other the limited, non-managing interest. Effectively, each member would hold dual classes of interest in the LLC, and the tax savings would come from the distributive share of income for the limited interest. While this approach is more technically correct than other strategies, it can be costly to set up correctly and a little impractical for smaller LLCs. On the other hand, since the proposed regulations are considered substantial authority, following them does protect LLC members from substantial underpayment penalties in the event of an audit adjustment.

The Reasonable Guaranteed Payment Approach

The most common self-employment minimization strategy for multi-member LLCs is to pay a guaranteed payment, which is subject to self-employment tax, to members providing services at a reasonable or determinable amount based on the services provided. Any distributive share of income above the guaranteed payment amount would therefore not be subject to self-employment tax and be structured as a return on investment like a limited member would expect to receive. If your spouse is the other member in your LLC and a limited partner for self-employment purposes, then the tax savings are even better. Just make sure that your lawyer prepares all the documentation needed to support the position.

Since there is no authoritative guidance for this approach, there is some audit risk involved with this type of strategy, but the risk is more about the uncertainty surrounding the argument that the IRS will use in an audit situation. You should definitely meet with your tax professional, and if it is still a concern, you could always elect to be treated as a corporation and then elect S status (see chapter 9 for details on the election), as there is much more authoritative guidance on this issue for the S corporation.

Tax Advantage Over the S Corporation

When comparing the LLC self-employment tax minimization strategies to the S corporation reasonable compensation strategy, it is important to know that the S corporation pays state unemployment tax on the reasonable wage paid to the shareholder, but the LLC guaranteed payment is not subject to the tax. While it is not a large tax, it has become more substantial in recent years in most states, so it is a factor to consider if you are comparing the entities.

BASIS FOR LLC MEMBERS

In order to deduct any distributed losses at year-end, each member needs sufficient basis in an LLC, which is a running balance that essentially tracks the member's investment in the LLC and their share of LLC liabilities. While LLC members do not need to have an in-depth understanding of basis, they should understand the basics so that they can anticipate the tax treatment of losses.

In some ways, LLCs and S corporations are similar when it comes to basis calculation, so make sure you read the shareholder basis section in chapter 9, as it will provide a foundation for this section. However, there are also sharp contrasts between LLCs and S corporations on basis calculation. For starters, a member's share of an increase in LLC liabilities generally increases a member's basis. This is a huge advantage over the S corporation, as its shareholders do not get any basis increase for debt in the corporation's name. Secondly, LLC basis is much more complex than S corporation basis as there are two levels of basis to consider. *Inside basis* is the LLC's adjusted basis in its assets, while *outside basis* is the member's adjusted basis in their LLC interest.

If you are feeling confused, do not worry, as your tax professional is the one who has to calculate your basis. Nonetheless, if you are expecting a business loss, you should start keeping track of what you have invested in the LLC and your share of LLC liabilities on an ongoing basis. Also, meet with your tax professional before year-end so that you do not have an unwelcome tax surprise near April 15. There is nothing worse than having a bad year and then finding out in the eleventh hour that you cannot deduct the loss.

Basis Calculation Basics

As long as members of an LLC do not contribute encumbered property, basis is fairly straightforward to calculate. Like the S corporation, your initial basis would be any funds contributed to the LLC or the basis of any property transferred into the LLC. The difference is that in LLCs, loans from a member are generally not separately accounted for, as these amounts would simply be part of the member's capital balance. At the end of the first tax year, your share of the following items would increase your initial basis:

- ordinary net income,

- separately stated income items, and

- increases in LLC liabilities.

After adding the above amount to your initial basis, the following items would then reduce your basis balance:

- decreases in LLC liabilities,

- non-deductible expenses,

- separately stated deductions, and

- net ordinary business losses.

In addition to the above distributed items, basis would be increased by any additional member capital contributions and reduced by any member draws, which are simply withdrawals of earnings by the member that are similar to S corporation distributions. The remaining balance, if any, would be your basis at year-end and then the process would be repeated each tax year.

If a member has insufficient basis at year-end, any disallowed losses are carried forward until future tax years when basis is restored. Like with S corporations, there are ordering rules and non-deductible expenses have to be deducted before business losses in the basis calculation (refer to the shareholder basis section in chapter 9), so significant meals and entertainment expenses can cut into your allowed losses.

Causes of Disallowed Member Losses

LLC members typically do not run out of basis as much as S corporation shareholders do, and that is because LLC members get basis from their share of LLC liabilities and S corporation shareholders generally do not. The items that cause the basis problems in LLCs are member capital contributions and draws, which are usually going to be different for each member. For example, if one member leaves a majority of their capital and earnings within the company while the other draws most of their capital out of the LLC, the latter member could end up with disallowed losses, as they were essentially funded by the other member's capital left in the LLC. The result in this type of scenario is fair, but it can be a surprise to the member with the disallowed losses if they are not paying attention to their draws relative to the taxable loss and cash flow.

Basis Recordkeeping

Even though the tax professional preparing the LLC tax return should provide members with a basis statement along with the Schedule K-1, members are ultimately responsible for keeping track of basis, so make sure the basis statements are kept each year. Also, if a different tax professional prepares your personal tax return, make sure they are tracking your basis and double-checking the basis statement from the other preparer. Occasionally, tax preparers make mistakes with LLC basis statements since there are two levels of basis,

---

LLC Advantage

Unlike S corporation distributions, LLC draws do not have to be proportionate to ownership, which not only provides accounting and tax simplification, but also brings great flexibility among members.

---

but the tax preparer of your personal tax return has to make the final determination since they are actually claiming the loss on your return.

Late Filing Penalties

If you fail to file an extension for your 1065 tax return or you file after the extended deadline of September 15, you will undoubtedly receive a late filing penalty notice with a large amount due from the IRS. The penalty is $195 per member, per month late, so it can add up very quickly to several thousand dollars in non-deductible penalties owed to the IRS. Fortunately, there is an automatic abatement procedure for the penalty that is fairly easy and painless. In fact, all you have to do is affirmatively answer the following questions:

- Is the partnership a domestic partnership?

- Does the partnership have ten or fewer partners? Husbands and wives and their estates are treated as one partner for this purpose.

- Are all partners natural persons (other than a nonresident alien) or an estate of a deceased partner?

- Is each partner's share of each partnership item the same as their share of every other item?

- Have all the partners timely filed their income tax returns?

- Have all the partners fully reported their share of the income, deductions, and credits of the partnership on their timely filed income tax returns?

If you can affirmatively answer each of these questions for your LLC taxed as a partnership, then all you need to do is write a quick letter requesting abatement under Rev. Proc. 84-35 and affirm each of these questions above. Most tax professionals have a quick form letter they can put together for you with all the correct language, so make sure to contact them as soon as you receive a notice like this.

If you cannot affirmatively answer all the above questions, then hopefully you have reasonable cause for the late filing. Otherwise, it is unlikely that the IRS will abate the penalty. However, do not give up if denied after the initial letter as the IRS service centers are very large, and often you can find someone sympathetic to your case if you are respectful and persistent in pleading your case.

S Corporations Do Not Have Automatic Abatement

This abatement procedure under Rev. Proc. 84-35 does not apply to S corporation late filing penalties. Unfortunately, the S corporation late filing penalties were created after the partnership penalties, and for some reason they never got around to issuing similar revenue procedures for S corporations. Refer to chapter 9 for more information on this disadvantage for S corporations.

PART III
Maximizing Your Deductions

Chapter 11

MAXIMIZING YOUR DEDUCTIONS

One of the biggest myths out there regarding small business taxation is the misconception that there are secret deductions out there to uncover that will instantly save you thousands of dollars, and that subscribing to a newsletter or buying a book will magically unlock them for you to claim. This type of mentality should come as no surprise given our culture of instant gratification and quick solutions. After all, who wouldn't want any easy solution when it comes to a confusing subject like taxes? While it may be tempting when a slick marketer claims that a one-time payment to them will instantly unlock dozens of deductions for you, it is important that you understand that real tax deduction maximization requires much more work than that.

THE CORRECT WAY TO
MAXIMIZE YOUR DEDUCTIONS

If you want to maximize your deductions and minimize your tax liability the correct way, you need to actually dig in and learn the rules and exceptions for the major deductions that small business owners regularly incur. Once you have a good, basic understanding of the rules, then you need to examine your specific circumstances so that you can develop strategies with your tax professional that work best within your business. This is a much better approach than paying for a number of hand-selected strategies and trying to make them fit your circumstances.

This chapter and the following chapters in Part III of this book are all designed to teach you the rules and exceptions that every small business owner should understand for the most popular deductions available today. This chapter covers some of the more basic tax deductions, while the following chapters in Part III cover the more complex deductions, which include:

- Vehicle deductions
- Travel expenses
- Meals and entertainment
- Retirement plans
- The office in home deduction
- Tax benefits for employers
- Family employee payroll

In order to get the most out of these chapters, make sure you have read the first two parts of this book, as they provide the groundwork for understanding this important information.

What Is Deductible?

The most frequent questions from new small business owners are typically in regards to what deductions they can claim against their business income, and if you have never owned a business, these are valid questions. The way I approach this is to pull out the tax form they will be filing or a sample chart of accounts for their industry, and simply go through the significant deductions and explain the special rules and complexities. This chapter takes that approach with a variety of common expenses that have special tax rules, but are still fairly straightforward and basic.

Advertising

Whether you invest in traditional advertising like telephone directory ads or more cutting edge advertising on social media sites, most reasonable advertising costs that are ordinary and necessary for your business are deductible. Business cards, advertisements in printed media, TV and radio spots, online ads, packaging design, and other similar costs are all deductible. However, there are a couple of advertising costs that require special attention.

Signs

If you purchase signage that will last longer than one year and has a material cost, you may need to capitalize the cost and depreciate it. This would be signage of a more permanent nature that is made of materials like metal and plastic.

Website Costs

For most businesses these days, their website is their most important advertisement to the general public and potential customers; however, the IRS has been surprisingly slow at addressing the issue of how to deduct these costs. Immaterial costs like domain registration, webhosting fees, and design update costs are clearly ordinary deductible expenses, but what about large design costs? I have had some clients pay $25,000 or more in design costs for complex websites and online storefronts. Also, what about large purchases of existing domains? Clients often purchase successful domain names from other businesses or online sellers for $5k to $10k. These large design and domain purchase costs most likely need to be amortized, so make sure you discuss these type of transactions with your tax professional so that you understand the tax impact they will have.

Donated Services

Often businesses will provide free services for public events or non-profit organizations in order to create goodwill for the business. For some reason business owners often think they should be given a deduction for these free services. While you can deduct any actual costs incurred, you cannot assign a cost to your time or expense what you would normally have been paid. Depending on how your business is structured, you probably already receive a salary, so extra work preformed does not create an extra expense whether it is donated or part of normal invoiced work. If you have employees provide free services, you are already deducting the cost of their wages, so there is no new expense created. Really it is a classification issue, and most of the time it is not worth reclassifying these costs to advertising expense.

Bad Debts

Unfortunately, non-paying customers or clients are an ordinary part of doing business, and while we try do our best to minimize uncollectable accounts, eventually you get to a point where, after making every reasonable attempt to collect the debt, you have to write-off an accounts receivable account.

A bad debt exists when, based on the facts and circumstances, there is no longer any reasonable expectation of payment. You should be able to prove that you took reasonable steps to collect the debt, so make sure you keep documentation supporting your collection efforts.

If you file your tax returns on the cash basis of accounting, there is generally no deduction available for bad debts, as you do not record sales until they are collected. Bad debt expenses are offsets to amounts previously recorded as income, so if there was never a sale recorded in the first place, you cannot claim a bad debt expense for tax purposes. If you self-prepare your cash basis tax returns, make sure you do not input an amount on the bad debt line as this can be a red flag to the IRS if it is a material amount.

If you file your tax returns on the accrual basis of accounting, you can claim a bad debt expense for any uncollectable accounts. You should review an accounts receivable aging report on a regular basis for uncollectable accounts so that you do not miss out on this deduction. If you later receive payments on an account you wrote off, they are recorded as bad debt recovery income.

If you loan funds to a supplier, client, business, or business partner and the loan becomes uncollectable, then a deduction is available whether on cash or accrual basis; however, to minimize audit risk, businesses on the cash basis should still avoid reporting the loss on the bad debt expense line. Also, make sure the loan was not to a relative or friend and there was an expectation of repayment.

Insurance
From basic liability insurance to workers compensation, insurance expenses are a necessity for businesses and generally deductible. However, there are a few important exceptions that small business owners need to understand.

First of all, life insurance premiums for owners of a business are generally not deductible to the business. Granted, there are some very complex life insurance products out there can be structured differently, but most standard term and whole life policies taken out on the life of the business owner are not deductible. Considering the fact that the proceeds received upon the passing of the business owner would not be taxable, it makes sense that these premiums would not be deductible. Make sure you clearly separate life insurance premiums in your accounting records or just pay the policies personally.

Health insurance expenses paid for employees are deductible by all types of business entities, but health insurance for a self-employed owner or a more than 2 percent S corporation shareholder are not deductible on the entity level and are instead deducted on the owner's 1040 tax return. Unless your business is organized as a C corporation, make sure you split out owner and employee health insurance in your accounting records.

Mobile Phones

Remember the large, grey cell phones in the late eighties that were the size of a brick? Even the early Motorola phones that were smaller look like antiques now. Obviously, much has changed over the last twenty years or more, and fortunately the IRS has finally updated its rules on cell phones.

The original tax rules on cell phones originated in 1989 when cell phones sold for $2,500 to $3,500 and were considered a novelty, as very few people owned them. At that time, the IRS designated cell phones as listed property, which means they were subject to strict recordkeeping rules that required a business owner to keep detailed documentation proving the business use percentage. If business use fell below 50 percent, special depreciation and deduction rules applied.

New Substantiation Rules

In January 2010, the IRS temporarily suspended enforcing strict substantiation rules on cell phones, and then in the 2010 Small Business Jobs Act, the listed property designation was removed altogether for cell phones. This change is effective for tax years beginning after December 31, 2009, and while this simplifies recordkeeping for the cell phone deduction, you still need to be sure that the cell phone is being used primarily for business if you are taking the full deduction. For some industries this is easy to meet, but if you are in an office all day and primarily use the office phone, then you may still want to only claim a portion of your cell phone use as business use.

Smartphone Use

If you use a smartphone for business, be cautious with the business use that is claimed for taxes, as these devices are much more complex and have much more potential for personal use than cell phones that only offer voice and text services. You may use your voice services primarily for business, but maybe your data plan usage is primarily for Facebook and watching YouTube videos. Alternatively, maybe you use the data plan primarily for business emails and social media, while your voice plan is used primarily for calls to family and friends. In either case, you should calculate the business use for the data plan separately from the voice plan—especially since the services are usually billed separately.

Rent

Rent paid to third parties for your office, warehouse, or other business location is deductible. Maintenance, utility and tax charges paid with rent are also deductible. If your business pays rent to you personally as the business owner, there are additional considerations and tax rules that you need to understand.

Self-Charged Rent

If you rent property to an active business of which you are an owner and material participant, you need to be aware that any net rental income resulting from the rental can generally not be offset against other passive rental losses you may have from other properties. Unlike normal rental net income that would be considered passive, the IRS requires self-charged

---

Example

Nick is a successful dentist with a profitable S corporation, but unfortunately he is not as successful with his five rental properties located throughout the Chicago area. Nick also owns the Teduski building in Chicago, which his dental practice rents from him at a reasonable rental amount. The five rental properties all generate passive losses, which cannot be deducted and can only be offset against other passive income. Even worse, the net rental income from the Teduski building cannot be offset against these passive rental losses, as the income has to be re-characterized as non-passive income.

---

rental income to be re-characterized as non-passive. While your tax professional should report this correctly when they prepare your individual tax return, small business owners need to be aware of this rule—especially those with other rental properties.

Repairs and Maintenance

Costs incurred to keep an asset in efficient operating condition are generally deductible as current expenses. However, major repairs that materially increase the value or extend the useful life of property are generally capitalized and depreciated as improvements. This is discussed in more detail in the Repairs vs. Improvements section in chapter 4.

Start Up Expenses

Starting a business is very expensive, and most of the time business owners have to pay for a fair amount of expenditures before the business activity begins. Unfortunately, many new business owners do not understand the IRS rules on start up costs and some miss out on substantial tax savings.

Currently, if total start up expenses are $50,000 or less, you can take an immediate deduction of $5,000 when the business starts and then the rest is amortized over 180 months. Once the total start up expenses exceed $50,000, the immediate deduction starts to phase out until it is completly phased out at $55,000. In 2010, the immediate deduction was temporarily increased to $10,000, but the temporary increase was never extended.

Start up expenses would include items that would normally be deductible if your business was operating at the time you incurred the expenses. Example of start up expenses would be pre-opening costs, investigatory costs, training expenses, advertising and travel costs required to line up vendors, distributors and customers. Capital expenditures or costs of acquiring a business or franchise would not be included.

In order to maximize your deductions, try to minimize the start up period by opening or starting your business sooner than later—especially if your start up expenses are reaching the $50k mark. 180 months is a long time over which to amortize expenses, so it is to your advantage to open your business before incurring more than $5k in start up expenses. That way nothing is amortized and the entire amount of start up expenses can be immediately deducted.

Make sure you discuss start up expenses with your tax professional, as an election will need to be filed with your tax return.

Supplies

Any consumable supplies used in the ordinary course of business are generally deductible, but if you make or buy goods to sell, you have to make sure the amounts you expense are general operating supplies and not supplies that should be part of cost of goods sold. Refer to chapter 3 for more on what costs should be included in cost of goods sold.

Taxes & Licenses

Small businesses pay a wide variety of taxes, licenses and fees to a multitude of state and local agencies, some of which are just for the right of doing business in a particular area. It is important to clearly separate your tax and license payments in your accounting records and watch for nondeductible amounts.

Deductible taxes and licenses include property taxes (both real and personal), state and local income taxes, payroll taxes, and annual registration fees and licenses. Sales taxes that you collect are only deductible if you also include collected taxes and part of income. Non-deductible amounts would include penalties charged for late payment of taxes or fines imposed by a governmental agency.

Chapter 12

Vehicle Deductions

"Keep Portland Weird" is a popular bumper sticker in my hometown of Soccer City, USA, and it is very fitting as we have a very unique city full of quirky people and an abundance of food carts, breweries, flannel, and very avid cyclists. In fact, we are rated one of the top cities for cyclists, and there are a growing number of inhabitants that only use a bike and mass transit. If you fit into this group and do not use a vehicle for business transportation, this chapter will likely not help you find any new deductions. However, for the majority of us that require a vehicle for business transportation needs, this chapter is a must read as automobile tax deductions are often an area of great confusion for small business owners.

This chapter provides detailed information that will help clear up any confusion and dispel any incorrect or bad advice you have been given in this area. It will also provide you with many strategies to maximize your vehicle deductions without driving up your audit risk. Even if you have been a business owner for many years, you will likely walk away with something new from this chapter.

What Qualifies as Business Use of a Vehicle?

Unfortunately, business use is much more complex than putting a decal advertising your business on your personal vehicle. For most vehicles, there actually has to be a business purpose for each use of the vehicle that is to be deductible, and you actually have to document the specifics of the business use in order to support your deduction. This is due to the fact that most vehicles are personal in nature, and so you have to essentially prove the portion of use that is business use. For each business trip, you should be able to document the reason why the trip was ordinary and necessary for your business. For businesses that use vehicles as a primary tool in providing their service, the business purpose is clear and it is entirely possible for business use to be close to or at 100 percent. However, businesses that require very little vehicle use in providing their product or service really have to be careful in their documentation and establishing business purpose for their trips. More importantly, they need to make sure they understand the difference between business miles, commuting miles, and personal miles.

Exception to the rule

Qualified Non-Personal Use Vehicles—there are trucks and vans that, due to their design and purpose, are not likely to be used more than a minimal amount for personal purposes. These would include vehicles with special modifications such as permanent shelving and painted exterior advertising. Delivery trucks with seating for only the driver, or only the driver and a folding jump seat would qualify as non-personal use vehicles. These vehicles require less substantiation and are generally assumed to be at 100 percent business use.

MAXIMIZING YOUR BUSINESS MILES

The IRS rules on what constitutes business miles are more confusing than you would think, and this is due to the fact that most small business owners misunderstand commuting miles and the principal place of business. The qualifications of a home office for purposes of vehicle deductions are fairly complex and restrictive, so simply setting up an office in your home does not instantly help you avoid commuting miles.

Commuting Miles
Whether you are an employee or self-employed, the first trip from your personal residence to your principal place of business, and the last trip back home from your principal place of business to your personal residence are non-deductible personal commuting costs. This would also include mass transit costs or any other method of transportation. The distance between your home and your principal place of business makes no difference—you cannot deduct these personal commuting costs. Commuting miles do not include miles driven when traveling away from home, as these miles would be travel expenses, which are covered in chapter 13.

Commuting miles are bad news for a business with a primary business location that is not located in the home, as these miles are usually a significant portion of total miles driven in an average year. In such a case, the only miles that would qualify as business miles would be the trips from the primary business location to temporary work locations or other destinations that have a business purpose, which may not amount to all that much in certain industries. If you have not noticed already, the tax deductions rules for business use of vehicles heavily favor single-owner service businesses that operate from their homes. However, all hope is not lost for the rest of us. There are still ways to maximize your auto deduction—it just requires an understanding of the office in home rules and exceptions with regard to the principal place of business.

Principal Place of Business

The specific rules for the office in home deduction and the principal place of business requirement are covered in detail in chapter 16, but essentially a home office must be used regularly and exclusively for a trade or business, and it must be the principal place of business unless several exceptions apply. This principal place of business requirement is the crucial element for the business vs. commuting miles issue, as the distance between your home and your principal place of business determines your commuting miles, and if you can reduce your daily commute from fifteen miles to the ten feet from your kitchen to your office, you can substantially reduce your tax liability.

Exceptions to the Rule

To qualify as the principal place of business, a home office must generally be the only place where substantial administrative and management activities are conducted. Unfortunately, small business owners who have a main commercial office and a home office have a very hard time meeting this requirement. However, there are two exceptions available to the principal place of business requirement that could help eliminate commuting miles:

- if you physically meet with clients, patients, or customers in your home office, and it is substantial and integral to your business, or

- your home office is a separate structure from the dwelling unit.

Meeting either of these two exceptions will qualify your office in home even though it is not the principle place of business, and more importantly, it will make your mileage from the home office to the other business office deductible as business miles. This can create significant tax savings, but you have to make sure you have a solid position as this issue will come up if an IRS auditor knocks at your door. First of all, make sure you are meeting with a significant amount of clients, patients, or customers in your home office on a regular basis. Otherwise, it will likely not qualify as substantial and integral to your business. Secondly, if your home office is a separate structure; make sure it is large enough to actually perform work in. I have personally been through audits where the IRS examined the separate structure, so do not even try claiming that messy tool shed in the backyard.

Regular Place of Business Argument

Lastly, some tax professionals believe that the principal place of business requirement is not necessary in order to deduct miles from a home office as long as it is the "regular place of business." They often refer to the *Walker* court case (101 TC 537 (1993)) in which a logger, who did not meet the principle place of business requirement, was allowed to deduct mileage from his residence—where he repaired and maintained equipment—to multiple locations in the forest. While it could probably be used for business owners with similar circumstances, it is a bit of a stretch to apply it to business owners providing personal services at a primary location and also from a secondary home office. Plus, having only one court case in your favor is not going to give you a strong position against the IRS and Revenue Ruling 94-47, not to mention the many court cases they could use. Using one of the exceptions to the principle place of business requirement is a much better position to take and will greatly minimize your audit risk.

Trip Planning and Minimizing Personal Miles

In addition to minimizing your commuting miles, planning your trips is also an important part of maximizing your business miles. With most vehicles, personal miles are necessary and unavoidable, and unfortunately they can greatly reduce the business use percentage for a vehicle—especially in this recessionary economy where many families are trying to downsize to one vehicle. However, if small business owners just spend a little extra time planning their trips, personal miles can be minimized by making sure the primary purpose of your trips is business. If you leave from the office to go buy some office supplies, and you happen to stop briefly along the way to get a few personal items at the store, it is still a business trip as long as buying the office supplies was the primary purpose and the personal items purchased were just picked up along the way. Keep in mind, you have to keep this reasonable, and it should be fairly clear that the business purpose is the primary purpose of the trip. In other words, you are pushing it too far if you pick up a pencil at the office supply store every time you leave the house, or if you drive to a business meeting and then proceed 150 miles to the beach because it was "on the way." You get the point—be a pig, not a hog.

How Is the Vehicle Deduction Calculated?

Now that you understand what qualifies as business use of a vehicle and how to maximize your business miles, we need to look at the actual methods of calculating the vehicle deduction. There are two different methods that the IRS allows for calculating vehicle deductions: the standard mileage method and the actual expense method. You cannot use both methods on the same vehicle, and there are many different rules to consider based on the number of business vehicles you use and the type of vehicle. We will examine each method and then go through the exceptions and special rules that you should be aware of as a small business owner.

Actual Expense Method

The actual expense method is just that—all the actual expenses and out-of-pocket costs of operating your vehicle for your business. This would include gas, repairs, insurance, oil changes, tires, towing, registration fees, loan interest, and any other similar expenses. In addition, you can claim depreciation if you own the vehicle, which will be discussed later in this chapter, or expense the lease payments if you lease. All these expenses would be totaled and multiplied by the business use percentage, which is calculated by dividing the business miles into the total miles driven during the year, which includes personal and commuting miles. This means that you still have to keep a mileage log or some form of contemporaneous documentation in order to support the business use percentage claimed.

Under the actual expense method, parking fees are fully deductible regardless of the business use percentage for the vehicle; however, this would not include parking fees at your regular place of work as these are personal commuting expenses. Also, parking tickets, or any other type of tickets, are non-deductible—even if received in the course of business. Vehicle loan interest is deductible at the percentage of business use, and the non-business use portion would be non-deductible personal interest. As you can imagine, tracking all these expenses in your accounting systems and splitting them out can be a daunting task for some small business owners, so the IRS devised a second option that simplifies reporting.

The Standard Mileage Method

Instead of tracking each vehicle expense, a simplified method is available—unless specifically excluded—that only requires the small business owner to keep track of business miles and total miles for the vehicle. The business miles are then multiplied by a standard mileage rate that changes each year (sometimes twice a year when the IRS feels there is not enough complication in the Code). For 2012, the standard business mileage rate is 55.5 cents a mile.

The standard mileage rate includes an allowance for depreciation and normal operating expenses, so you cannot deduct actual auto expenses in addition to claiming a deduction using the standard mileage method for the same vehicle. Then again, this is the IRS we are talking about, so there are several exceptions to this rule. Like with the actual expense method, you can claim the full amount of any parking fees in addition to the standard mileage allowance. You can also deduct the business use portion of any vehicle loan interest and any property taxes paid on the vehicle.

To use the standard mileage rate for a vehicle you own, you must choose to use the method in the first year the vehicle is available for use in your business. You cannot revoke the choice, but you can switch to the actual expense method later. The only catch is that you can only depreciate the vehicle using the straight-line method over the remaining useful life of the vehicle, which is substantially less than the depreciation that would have been available had you used the actual method from the beginning. If you are leasing your vehicle and want to use the standard mileage method, you have to use the method for the entire term of the lease.

When the Standard Mileage Method Is Not an Option

The IRS does not allow use of the standard mileage method if the following applies to your business:

- You used the actual expense method on the same vehicle in prior years and used MACRS depreciation, a 179 deduction, or a special depreciation allowance,

- you lease or own five or more cars and use them "at the same time" in your business, or

- you are a rural mail carrier who received a qualified reimbursement.

The key here is that if you start using the actual expense method with some form of accelerated depreciation, then you cannot take the standard mileage deduction in a later year for the same vehicle. If you have multiple vehicles, make sure you keep track of the method used for each so that you record the information that will be needed at tax time to calculate your deduction. If you get to a point where you have five or more business vehicles that are used at the same time (like a fleet of trucks used in a landscaping company), you will have to start using the actual expense method for any car used by the business. Why did the IRS pick five vehicles as the limit? I suppose six would not work and seven was out of the question, so we are stuck with a five vehicle rule—no more, no less. Most IRS rules like this are about as ridiculous as the Holy Hand Grenade of Antioch; however, based on recent developments, the IRS is looking into the need for this rule.

WHICH METHOD PROVIDES
THE LARGER DEDUCTION?

What method provides a larger deduction ultimately depends on your circumstances. You have to look at how many business miles you drive each year, the projected vehicle expenses, your vehicle's gas mileage and your projected business use. Sales people and real estate agents that drive a significant amount of miles for their business can sometimes benefit more from the standard mileage rate. On the other hand, vehicles with poor gas mileage, like large SUVs, are prime candidates for the actual expense method, and you can generally depreciate them more quickly.

For leased vehicles, the actual expense method will generally give you a larger deduction, which is simply due to the way lease rates are established and how the numbers work out. Plus, the fact that you have to stay with the standard mileage method for the life of the lease is a fairly significant disadvantage.

The standard mileage rate usually works best for vehicles that are used casually for business or have less than 50 percent business use. This is especially true for the second family vehicle that the owner's spouse occasionally uses for the business.

Depreciation and Disposal Considerations

You also have to consider the depreciation rules available at the time of the purchase. In recent years, special bonus depreciation has been available for new car purchases, so the actual expense method usually provided a better initial depreciation deduction. We will discuss depreciation of vehicles in more depth later in this chapter, but given all the recent changes to depreciation tax rules and how temporary the tax code is right now, you should always talk to your tax professional before purchasing a vehicle in order to maximize your deduction. Often small details like purchase date and vehicle type can mean thousands in extra tax savings for you.

Lastly, you have to consider disposition issues and the effect of any gains or losses that would be incurred upon sale or disposal of the vehicle. We will look at the disposition rules in more detail near the end of this chapter, but it is crucial to understand that there is still a gain or loss upon sale of a vehicle that you used the standard mileage rate on. Part of the mileage rate includes an amount of deemed depreciation, which you actually have to subtract from the vehicle's basis each year, so you could end up with a gain or loss that could substantially change the overall deduction for the vehicle.

All Vehicles Are Not Treated Equally

Up until this point, we have steered clear of the fact that there are many different types of vehicles and many special rules and exclusions that the IRS has for each type of vehicle.

Well, now that you understand the methods used for calculating vehicle deductions, it is time to add the next layer of complication and examine how the IRS categorizes vehicles.

Trucks

The IRS treats trucks, especially heavy trucks, more favorably as the first-year depreciation available is substantial. In fact, in most cases, a heavy truck can be expensed in full in the first year. For tax purposes, a truck has to have a bed of six feet or longer. Trucks with beds less than six feet are classified as "SUVs" for tax purposes.

The IRS categorizes trucks in the following groups:

- **Heavy truck**—a truck with a gross vehicle weight rating (GVWR) of over 6,000 pounds. Under current rules, these trucks are eligible to be expensed in the year of purchase regardless of whether new or used.

- **Light truck**—a truck with a GVWR of 6,000 pounds or less. These trucks are often described as "luxury trucks", as they are subject to the luxury depreciation limits, which greatly reduces the first year deduction—particularly if the light truck is used.

Vans

Next to trucks, the IRS treats vans quite favorably—especially if they meet one of the three requirements below from IRC 179(b)(5)(B)(ii):

- seating capacity of more than nine persons behind the driver's seat (passenger van),

- a cargo area of at least six feet in interior length which is an open area or is designed for use as an open area but is enclosed by a cap and is not readily accessible directly from the passenger compartment, or

- an integral enclosure, fully enclosing the driver compartment and load carrying device, no seating reward of the driver's seat, and no body section protruding more than thirty inches ahead of the leading edge of the windshield (cube or cargo van).

If a van meets one of these requirements, and it has a GVWR of over 6,000 pounds, it qualifies as a van for tax purposes and qualifies for full first-year depreciation under Section 179. If a van fails to meet any of the requirements, it is treated as an SUV for tax purposes.

SUVs

The IRS's SUV category is actually much broader than vehicles we would consider SUVs. This is due to the fact that trucks with beds less than six feet and vans that fail to meet any of the three requirements discussed earlier fall into this category. Like trucks, SUVs fall into two categories based on GVWR:

- **Heavy SUV**—these vehicles have a GVWR of over 6,000 pounds and can be depreciated more quickly. Before 2004, you could fully expense them in the year of purchase like with heavy trucks, but Congress closed the loophole in 2004 and now your Section 179 deduction is limited to $25k. If it is a new vehicle, bonus depreciation can be more than the $25k limit, but it depends on the year of purchase (discussed in the next section).

- **Light SUV**—these vehicles are subject to the luxury depreciation limits, like the light trucks, as they have a GVWR of 6,000 or less.

The light SUV and light truck are basically treated like passenger cars for tax purposes, and the depreciation options are not as generous as those available for heavy trucks, SUVs, and vans that meet IRS requirements.

Passenger Cars

This is the catch-all category for all vehicles that do not meet the requirements to be classified as trucks, vans, or SUVs. Basically, if they have four wheels and a GVWR of 6,000 pounds or less, they likely fall in the passenger car category for tax purposes. The only exceptions would be vehicles used directly in the business of transporting persons or property for pay or hire; an ambulance, hearse, or combination ambulance-hearse (not a joke—see Publication 463); and certain qualified non-personal use vehicles.

Depreciation is significantly limited for the vehicles in this category because of the IRS luxury vehicle depreciation limits, which are inflation-indexed dollar limits set by the IRS each year that cap depreciation regardless of the cost of a vehicle. The limits actually have nothing to do with luxury vehicles, and unfortunately it is an area that needs tax reform as most average-priced vehicles can take up to eighteen years or more to be fully-depreciated under these rules. Like it or not, they are the rules, and if you do not want the low depreciation limits, then you have to make sure the vehicle you purchase is a heavy truck, van, or heavy SUV.

MAXIMIZING YOUR VEHICLE DEPRECIATION DEDUCTION

Now that you understand the four categories that the IRS groups vehicles into, it will be easier to discuss depreciation deductions for vehicles. We discussed the basics of depreciation and fixed assets in chapter 5, and as I mentioned in that chapter, depreciation is an area of the tax law that is

---

Important!

There are three different depreciation methods used for vehicles, but not every vehicle qualifies for each method. Also, keep in mind that for each of these methods, you can only claim the business use portion of the depreciation. The limits listed in the following sections are all based on 100 percent business use, so you will have to calculate the reduced depreciation based on your business use percentage. If business use does not exceed 50 percent, then Section 179 and bonus depreciation methods are not available.

---

constantly being changed and extended in yearly rounds of stimulus tax bills. For 2011 and 2012, there are very generous depreciation rules for vehicles, but much of that is scheduled to expire, so you should always check with your tax professional before purchasing a vehicle to make sure special provisions are still available.

Section 179 Depreciation

The Section 179 depreciation deduction is only available for purchases of new and used vehicles classified as:

- heavy trucks,
- vans, and
- heavy SUVs (although a $25k limit applies).

Except for the heavy SUV exception, the Section 179 deduction allows you to take the entire cost of the vehicle and expense it in the year of purchase, which can provide substantial tax savings in a very profitable year. If you can use a vehicle of this size in your business, this is definitely the best way to go.

Chapter 5 provides detailed information on the Section 179 depreciation deduction. Make sure you check with your tax professional on current 179 depreciation limits before purchasing the vehicle, as the limits are scheduled to be reduced to $25k in 2013 unless Congress extends the current limits. Also, remember that the vehicle has to be used predominately for business (more than 50 percent use) in order to qualify for Section 179 depreciation.

BONUS DEPRECIATION

Bonus depreciation is scheduled to expire after 2012, so unless Congress acts to extend the benefit, it will no longer be available for vehicles or any fixed assets for that matter. For 2012, bonus depreciation can be taken on new vehicle purchases up to 50 percent of the cost of the vehicle; however, the vehicle must be used predominately for business (more than 50 percent use). For more information on how this is calculated, refer to Chapter 5.

For heavy trucks and vans, Section 179 is still a better deal, but for expensive heavy SUVs, 50 percent bonus depreciation can provide a larger deduction than the $25k Section 179 limitation. However, bonus depreciation provides the best benefit for light trucks, light SUVs, and passenger cars, which are all subject to the luxury vehicle depreciation limits.

Luxury Vehicle Depreciation

As discussed earlier in the passenger car section, the luxury vehicle depreciation limits are dollar limits issued by the IRS each year that significantly limit depreciation on light trucks, light SUVs, and passenger cars. The luxury limits provide larger deductions in years one through three, but for year four and later, the deduction is fairly minimal, which can stretch out the depreciable life well past the useful life of the vehicle. The IRS issues two sets of limits each year—one for passenger cars and the other for light trucks and vans classified as light SUVs.

In recent years, bonus depreciation has greatly increased the luxury limits for new car purchases—especially in the first year. In 2012, 50 percent depreciation is available, but in 2013 bonus depreciation is scheduled to expire, so luxury limits will likely return to the low, nominal amounts that were in place before 2008. Below is a table showing the limits for 2007—2012. The IRS issues the limits in March or April of the tax year to which the limits apply.

Luxury Vehicle Depreciation Limits					
	For Passenger Cars				
Year Placed	New	Used			4th Year
in Service	1st Year	1st Year	2nd Year	3rd Year	and Later
2012	$ 11,160	$ 3,160	$ 5,100	$ 3,050	$ 1,875
2011	11,060	3,060	4,900	2,950	1,775
2010	11,060	3,060	4,900	2,950	1,775
2009	10,960	2,960	4,800	2,850	1,775
2008	10,960	2,960	4,800	2,850	1,775
2007	3,060	3,060	4,900	2,850	1,775
	For Trucks and Vans				
Year Placed	New	Used			4th Year
in Service	1st Year	1st Year	2nd Year	3rd Year	and Later
2012	$ 11,360	$ 3,360	$ 5,300	$ 3,150	$ 1,875
2011	11,260	3,260	5,200	3,150	1,875
2010	11,160	3,160	5,100	3,050	1,875
2009	11,060	3,060	4,900	2,950	1,775
2008	11,160	3,160	5,100	3,050	1,875
2007	3,260	3,260	5,200	3,050	1,875

The Two-Vehicle Tax Strategy

The luxury vehicle depreciation limits are dollar limit caps applied to each vehicle used for business. One way to get around the low limitation is to use two vehicles for business instead of one. If you have the right mix of circumstances, the strategy can greatly increase your vehicle deductions; however, it does require sitting down with your tax professional and factoring in the long-term tax consequences including eventual disposals.

The best scenario is usually where you have two vehicles of similar value and a business owner that drives a significant amount of business miles. Instead of driving most of the miles on one car and minimal miles on the other, alternating use of the vehicles so that they are equally used for business can not only give you much higher depreciation, but sometimes up to 30 to 40 percent more in overall deductions.

This two-vehicle strategy does not work for everyone and there can be negative consequences years later when you sell a vehicle, so be sure to spend some time on long-term tax planning with your tax professional before switching cars with your spouse.

Avoid Recapture

Depreciation recapture basically means you have to claim income for excess depreciation claimed in prior years. For vehicles, recapture usually results when business use drops below 50 percent, but it all depends on the type of depreciation that was claimed on the vehicle:

- **Section 179 depreciation**—recapture results in the year business use falls below 50 percent. Make sure you arrange your driving to avoid this outcome at all costs.

- **Bonus depreciation (non-luxury limits)**—surprisingly, there is no recapture on non-luxury limit vehicles that you claimed bonus depreciation on, which gives bonus depreciation for heavy trucks, vans, and heavy SUVs a major advantage over Section 179 depreciation if business use is a concern.

- **Bonus depreciation (luxury vehicles)**—recapture results in the year business use drops below 50 percent, which is calculated by making a retroactive change to the straight-line method and recapturing the excess deductions taken in prior years. Again, do whatever you can to avoid this.

DISPOSITION OF VEHICLES

Whether you trade-in business vehicles every few years or use them until they are worn out, eventually you will have to deal with the tax consequences for a disposition, which can result in a gain or loss depending on the circumstances. If you trade-in a vehicle, any gain or loss is deferred forward into the basis of the new replacement vehicle. This means that if you have a gain based on the trade-in value, the basis of the new vehicle will be reduced by the deferred gain on the old vehicle. If there was remaining debt on the old vehicle, the calculation can get a little complex and you will likely need your tax professional to walk you through the 1031 exchange calculations. However, most vehicle trade-ins are fairly straightforward. Eventually, if you were to sell the new vehicle rather than trade-in again, the deferred gain would finally be recognized.

If you sell a business vehicle outright, the gain or loss is the difference between the sales price and your adjusted basis, which is original cost less depreciation. Due to the fact that vehicles quickly depreciate in value, gains are unusual unless you took Section 179 or bonus depreciation in prior years. Always check with your tax professional before selling a business vehicle as they can calculate any gain or loss in advance.

Finally, if you used the standard mileage rate on the business vehicle, there could be a gain or loss depending on the amount of business miles used. A portion of the mileage rate is considered deemed depreciation, so you have to go back through the years the vehicle was in service and calculate the reduction to adjusted basis by multiplying the deemed depreciation rate by the business miles used. Below is a table of the rates for the past ten years. Many small business owners do not know about this rule, and sometimes it can even result in a loss, so make sure your tax professional runs the calculation for you.

Deemed Depreciation Rates	
Tax Year	Rate Per Mile
2012	23¢
2011	22¢
2010	23¢
2009	21¢
2008	21¢
2007	19¢
2006	17¢
2005	17¢
2004	16¢
2003	16¢

Chapter 13

TRAVEL EXPENSES

Even though online collaboration and video conferencing technology has in some way reduced the amount of business travel needed, many businesses still incur a fair amount of travel expenses in the ordinary course of their business. Regardless of whether it is a sales presentation, travel to an out-of-town temporary work assignment, or an annual business planning trip, it is important that every small business owner clearly understands the IRS rules on travel, as you will find that there are many opportunities to maximize your deductions by arranging your trip to work best within the rules.

In this chapter, you will learn what expenses qualify as travel, the specific rules for each type of travel expense, who you can deduct travel expenses for, and the specific rules for the different types of travel.

TRAVEL VS. LOCAL TRANSPORTATION EXPENSES

Like any tax deduction, the IRS requires travel expenses be both ordinary and necessary, and of course, it must be for your business, profession, or job. More specifically, it must be incurred when "traveling away from home." Before defining this requirement in detail, it is important to distinguish travel expenses from local transportation expenses and commuting costs.

Any normal commuting costs from your residence to your normal place of business would not be includible as travel expenses, nor would any transportation expenses to locations within the city or general area in which your business is located. For more information on these costs and expenses, refer to chapter 12, which covers vehicle and other transportation deductions. This chapter concentrates on travel to locations outside the city or general area in which your business is located.

What Is Considered Traveling Away From Home?

In order for a deduction to qualify as a travel expense, the IRS requires that you actually "travel away from home", but what does that mean? Well, according to IRS Publication 463, you are considered to be traveling away from home if:

- your duties require you to be away from the general area of your tax home "substantially longer than an ordinary day's work," and

- you need to sleep or rest to meet the demands of your work while away from home.

Unfortunately, this is typical of the IRS to provide answers that only leave you with more questions and terminology to look up. We will look at the definition of "tax home" shortly, but the basic idea here is that you have to be away from home long enough to warrant the need for sleep or rest. They do not come out and give an exact definition of how long you must be away, as it largely depends on the circumstances and the type of work involved. For most service businesses, a four hour meeting or convention in a city that is only one hour away would likely not meet the requirements for travel, however, an all-day seminar in a city three hours away would likely fit the bill. Nonetheless, the first requirement of it being "substantially longer than an ordinary day's work" should not be taken as meaning literally longer than a typical eight to five shift, as you do not necessarily need to be away the whole day. Your relief from duty just needs to be long enough to get the necessary sleep or rest required by your job.

Example

For a long haul truck driver, the need for sleep and rest between shifts is very important, and a six hour rest in the middle of a sixteen hour round trip may qualify as traveling away from home without a problem. On the other hand, a nap in the sleeper cabin for only an hour in-between trips would likely not qualify as traveling away from home.

The key to meeting these requirements and not putting your deductions at risk is reasonableness. If you are trying to stretch out a half-day seminar so that you can write off your meal and incidental costs, the audit risk is not worth the small amount of additional expense you may gain. Instead, put some planning into your business trips that clearly qualify as traveling away from home so that you can maximize your deductions with little to no audit risk.

WHERE IS YOUR TAX HOME?

To be considered traveling away from home, your duties have to require you to be away from the general area of your "tax home", but what is a tax home and how is it determined? Well, it is not necessarily where your family home or residence is located, although it can be if you operate from your home. According to the IRS, the location of your tax home is your regular place of business, and it includes the entire city or general area in which your business is located.

If you have more than one business location, you have to determine which location is your main place of business. In evaluating each location, you should look at the time you spend at each location, the level of business activity by location, and the income generated from each location. If you have no regular place of business due to the nature of your business, then your tax home defaults to the place where you regularly live. If there is no place where you regularly live and you basically live wherever you can find work, you are essentially kissing your travel expenses goodbye, as you are now a "transient" in the eyes of the IRS and not considered to be traveling away from home. This has actually become very common in this recessionary economy among contractors that live in trailers and move around the country wherever there is work, and it will be examined in more detail in this chapter in the temporary assignments section.

Regardless of your situation and circumstances, make sure you have a clear understanding of where your tax home is for purposes of the IRS travel rules. If you have a complicated situation, refer to publication 463 or talk to your tax professional to make sure your travel deductions would not be at risk in an audit situation.

What Is Deductible?

Now that you have a basic understanding of what the IRS considers travel, we need to look at the individual travel deductions that are deductible, how the costs should be separated, and what records should be kept to support your deductions. When going through the specific deductions, remember that the expenses must be ordinary and necessary and have a business purpose.

Transportation

Whether you travel by plane, train, or an automobile between your tax home and your business destination, you can generally deduct the costs of your ticket or fare. However, if you use your frequent flyer miles for a business trip, the deductible cost is unfortunately zero, so you might want to save them for that personal trip to Hawaii. If you prefer to travel on the open sea, there are special rules on the deductibility of trips on cruise ships and other luxury water transportation, which we discuss later in the chapter. Lastly, if you haven't found your sea legs and choose to travel on land using your business vehicle, you would just deduct your normal auto expenses using either the standard mileage rate or actual expenses. Refer to chapter 12 for more information on deducting these costs.

In addition to deducting your transportation costs to get to your destination, you can also deduct the cost of any local trips between the airport or station, your hotel, a business meeting place, a temporary work location, or a customer or client's location. Whether you choose a taxi or a limousine, it just has to be ordinary and necessary for your business and not lavish or extravagant. The cost of a rental car is also deductible, so now you can upgrade from economy to full size without feeling guilty. The only local transportation costs during your business trip that would not be deductible would be any costs for personal travel like sightseeing, shopping, or other non-business activities.

Lodging

If your business trip is overnight or long enough to require sleep and rest, then any lodging or other accommodation costs are generally deductible. Most small business owners have to deduct the actual cost of lodging and cannot use the lodging portion of federal per diem rate, which is a location-based standard allowance set by the IRS to cover lodging, meals and incidental expenses. Basically, the rules state that you are not eligible to use per diem for lodging if you are one of the following:

- self-employed (sole proprietor, partner in a partnership, or a member of an LLC),

- a ten percent shareholder of an S or C corporation (see Rev. Proc. 2011-47), or

- an employee related to a 10 percent shareholder under Code Sec. 267(b).

Most small business owners would likely fall into one of the above categories, so be sure to keep track of your actual lodging expenses like you would with your transportation costs. In addition, make sure you split out meal costs and other amounts spent for food and beverages, including the related taxes and tips on these costs, from the actual lodging costs. If a hotel does not provide this detail, you can reasonably allocate them. Splitting out these costs is very important as there are deduction limits placed on meals and entertainment expenses.

Note

If you are a shareholder who owns less than 10 percent of your business and you would like to find out more about the per diem method for lodging, refer to IRS Publication 1542. There are two components that make up the overall per diem rate: the lodging rate and the meals and incidentals rate. Publication 1542 lists rates by travel locality and also explains the alternative high-low method.

Meals

If you need to stop for substantial sleep or rest to properly perform you duties while traveling away from home, not only can you deduct lodging costs, but you can also deduct your meal costs. Normally, meals are only deductible if they are business-related entertainment, but when traveling away from home you can deduct meals without meeting this requirement. However, meals are subject to a 50 percent limit, which is why it is important to split out costs for lodging and meals. If you are subject to the Department of Transportation's "hours of service" limits, you actually get to deduct 80 percent of your meals and entertainment costs.

There are two methods available for figuring your meals expense: (1) actual cost and (2) the standard meal allowance. The actual cost of a meal includes food, beverages, taxes and tips, and under the actual cost method, you would need to keep records of the actual costs paid like with lodging and transportation costs. Alternatively, you can use the standard meal allowance, which is the meals and incidental expense portion of the federal per diem rate. Unlike the lodging per diem rules, there are no restrictions preventing self-employed individuals and ten percent corporate shareholders from using the meals and incidental allowance, so if it makes your recordkeeping easier to manage or gives you a larger deduction, you should definitely use it. However, keep in mind that:

- you still have to keep records to document the time, place and business purpose of your travel,

- both methods are subject to the 50 percent limitation (or 80 percent if "hour of service" limits are applicable), and

- the allowance includes incidentals expenses like fees, tips and shipping costs, so you cannot claim the allowance for meals and then claim actual incidental expenses.

For meals and incidental per diem rates, refer to IRS Publication 1542. It includes the rates by locality and details on the alternative high-low method.

Other Costs

If you do not use the per diem meals and incidental allowance, you can deduct the actual costs for other incidental travel costs. These costs would include:

- tips and fees given to porters, baggage carriers, bellhops, hotel maids, stewards, and any other workers that assist you during your travels,

- transportation costs between your place of lodging or business location and the places where you have your meals, and

- mailing costs related to sending travel vouchers and other travel documentation.

Incidental expenses do not include other expenses like dry cleaning and laundry expenses, lodging taxes, telephone and fax costs, and any other ordinary and necessary expenses not listed above that are incurred while traveling. The actual cost of these expenses can be deducted whether or not the meals and incidental allowance is used.

Expenses for a Spouse, Dependent, or Other Individual

Generally, you cannot deduct travel expenses for a spouse, dependent, or other individual if they travel with you on a business trip. However, the IRS makes an exception as long as all of the following are true:

- the other individual is your employee,

- a bona fide business purpose exists for the person to travel with you, and

- the other individual would otherwise be allowed to deduct the travel.

In addition to the above requirements, the individual cannot simply provide incidental services like note taking or acting as an assistant, so make sure they have a substantial role in the business purpose of the trip.

The Employee Requirement

If all business entities were corporations, there would be little to no confusion over this requirement since family members involved with a family-owned corporation would most likely all be employees. However, the popularity of non-corporate entities like the limited liability company has complicated this requirement, as these entities – taxed as partnerships – are not allowed to treat their owners as employees. Therefore, this requirement should not be taken literally for all business entity types. If your spouse or child is an LLC member or a partner in your business, then this rule does not preclude you from deducting their travel expenses.

Regardless of how you structure your business, it is crucial that the family member be a legitimate, active employee or self-employed owner involved in the operations of the business if you want to deduct their travel expenses. Family members cannot simply be employees by title. Make sure that they are actually providing services and receiving reasonable compensation for those services. If your spouse becomes an LLC member or partner in your business, make sure that you have a lawyer draft up supporting documents for the ownership purchase. Titles without documentation or economic substance can quickly become meaningless in an IRS audit, so do not take any shortcuts in trying to meet this requirement.

The Bona Fide Business Purpose Requirement

It is not enough that the spouse or family member traveling with you be an employee, there must also be a "bona fide" (or real) business purpose for the individual's presence. This business purpose must be substantial and be more than providing incidental services like typing notes or entertaining customers or clients. What qualifies as a real business purpose is going to be different depending on your industry and the circumstances surrounding your business, but as a general rule, your business purpose should hold up in audit as long as it is reasonable and well documented. For example, if you have an annual business planning trip in Hawaii for your small, family-owned business, make sure all those individuals for which you claim a deduction are actively involved in the planning sessions and that all the work done on the trip is documented. If you travel to a seminar or convention, make sure you are only deducting for individuals that are actually attending the event and that the content applies to their role in the business.

If your spouse, family members, or employees do not meet the requirement, then you will need to split out the deductible portion of the expenses for you from the non-deductible portion for them. As a basic rule, the deductible portion would be the amount of expense that would have been incurred if you traveled alone. For example, you could deduct lodging expenses equal to the cost of a single occupancy room, and if you drove to your destination, the full cost of the travel would be deductible, as you would have incurred that expense regardless of whether or not other individuals accompanied you in the vehicle. However, you cannot deduct any portion of a travel fare or meal for an individual that does not meet the requirement.

Traveling with Business Associates

In addition to employees, spouses, and children, you can deduct travel expenses for a business associate that traveled with you if they meet the bona fide business purpose requirement and if the travel expenses would otherwise be deductible. In other words, if you were not paying for their travel expenses, they would still be able to deduct their travel costs through their business. To qualify for this deduction, it has to be someone with whom you could reasonably expect to actively conduct business. It can be a current or prospective customer, supplier, client, employee, agent, partner, or advisor. Basically, this is a common sense rule for a common deduction that is often necessary in business. However, as you apply it to your business, use some reasonableness with the individuals you claim a deduction for—especially if they could be called a related party.

MANY WAYS TO TRAVEL, MANY DIFFERENT RULES

Whether you are traveling away from home for a temporary assignment or for a business planning trip, it is important to be aware of the rules that apply to each type of business travel. Use this section as a reference when planning your business trips so that you can maximize your tax deductions and avoid tax traps.

Temporary Assignments and Jobs

In the current recessionary economy, there are a lot of contractors that are working at temporary locations, sometimes far away from their home, for several months at a time. It is an industry that has been hit hard by the recession; so many have had to go wherever the work is available. Some workers come home each weekend to their family, while others have become mobile and live wherever there is work. Regardless of your situation, there are very specific rules regarding temporary assignments that need to be followed before you even start a temporary job.

Temporary Assignment Rules

First, the temporary assignment or job needs to be located in a place where it is not practical to return to your tax home at the end of each day. Otherwise, it would not be considered traveling away from your home. Secondly, the job needs to be one that is "realistically expected" to last for one year or less. If it is expected to last longer than one year, the job becomes indefinite according to the tax code and the job location becomes your new tax home, which means you cannot deduct travel expenses. This important determination needs to be made at the start of the job, and it becomes the deciding factor of deductibility—even in cases where the job ends early. If you realistically expect a temporary job to last less than one year and then the circumstances change that stretch the job beyond one year, you are only able to deduct travel expenses up to the point when the circumstances and facts changed.

If you go home on the weekends or on your days off, you cannot deduct your costs while you are home. However, you can deduct the travel and meal costs when traveling between the temporary location and your home up to the amount you would have paid for lodging and meals had you stayed at the temporary job location. If you keep your lodging while going home, you can deduct up to the meals that would have been incurred had you stayed.

Having No Tax Home Kills Deduction

Maintaining a tax home while working at a temporary assignment or job is crucial as you can lose your travel expenses altogether if you do not have a location—separate from your temporary work location—that is your regular place of business or the place where you regularly live. In this case, the IRS views you as a "transient" and you are not considered to be traveling away from home. While living in a trailer or RV that you travel to the temporary jobs in may save you money, it will definitely not save you any tax dollars. To avoid losing these deductions, you should try to arrange your affairs so that you can maintain a tax home without duplicating too many living expenses. If you have a hometown you return to on a regular basis, see if you can rent a room from a family member or somehow establish a place you regularly live. With that said, keep in mind that the tax rate is not 100 percent, and that sometimes the overall net cash effect is better without the tax savings from the travel deductions.

Business Travel in the United States

For business travel within the United States, the rules for determining what is deductible are fairly simplified as compared to foreign business travel. To determine the deductible portion of travel expenses for trips within the fifty states and the District of Columbia, you have to look at the primary purpose of the trip.

If your travel is entirely for business, all your costs would obviously be deductible, but what about trips that, while they are primarily related to business, include a personal side trip or other personal activities? Well, the answer is actually fairly straightforward. Essentially, you can deduct the travel costs to and from the business destination as well as any business-related travel expenses. The only costs that would not be deductible would be additional travel costs from the business destination to and from personal destinations and any personal expenses incurred. In other words, you do not need to pro-rate the travel costs to and from the business destination by the number of days used for personal activities as long as the primary purpose is for business.

If the primary purpose of your trip is personal, the entire cost of the trip is obviously nondeductible. However, you can

---

Example

Let's say that you are lucky enough to travel to Portland, Oregon, for a five-day business trip, and at the end of the week you take a quick one-day trip to Cannon Beach for a legendary bowl of clam chowder at Mo's Restaurant. Since the primary purpose of the overall trip to Portland is for business, you can deduct all the travel costs to and from Portland, the lodging, meals, and any other business costs incurred in Portland without having to pro-rate for the personal side trip. However, the cost of the rental car for that Cannon Beach day, gas, souvenirs, meals, and any other expenses related to the quick side trip would not be deductible.

---

deduct any expenses incurred while at your destination that are directed related to your business. That being said, minor business activities do not change a personal vacation into a business trip, so make sure you are clear about the primary purpose of your trips.

Foreign Travel

While the travel rules for trips within the United States are relatively simple, the rules on foreign travel are much more exacting and are written in a manner that requires an interpreter. I will try to keep it as simple as possible, but you should definitely talk to your tax professional before planning a foreign business trip as they can save you much more on a trip than a travel agent or discount travel website.

The IRS splits foreign travel into four different categories:

- Entirely for business
- *Considered* entirely for business
- Primarily for business
- Primarily for personal reasons

Entirely for Business

If you spend the entire time on business while traveling abroad, you can deduct all of your travel expenses. This is reasonable for short trips where there is no time for any personal activities; however, most foreign travelers would have a hard time not taking at least a day or two for some sightseeing, so realistically the IRS's first category would not apply to many businesses.

Considered Entirely for Business

Business travelers who do not spend their entire foreign trip on business can treat the travel expenses as entirely for business if they meet one of the four following exceptions:

- **No substantial control**—you did not have substantial control over arranging the trip (this only works for an employee who is unrelated to the employer and not a managing executive, so this is not an option for the small business owner).

- **Outside United States no more than a week**—you were only outside the US for a week or less (seven consecutive days, not counting the day you leave). In other words, keep it short and sweet and the trip will be fully deductible even if you do a little sightseeing.

- **Less than 25 percent of the time on personal activities**—if your trip lasts longer than a week, this exception should work for you as long as you spent less than 25 percent of the total time outside the United States on nonbusiness activities. For purposes of this exception, count both the day your trip began and the day it ended.

- **Vacation not a major consideration**—the last exception is fairly vague and not one I would suggest hanging your hat on, but if you can establish that a personal vacation was not a major consideration in your business trip, the trip can be considered entirely for business. Keep in mind that you would likely be trying to establish this to an auditor that sits in an office most of the time and doesn't travel much, so your best bet would be exception 2 or 3.

Primarily for Business

If your business trip does not meet any of the above exceptions and is not entirely for business, then you would fall into the IRS category of travel primarily for business. In this category, you have to allocate your travel expenses between business and non-business days of travel, which is calculated by dividing the total number of business days by the total days outside the United States. Even though it is a simple calculation, there are several rules you need to be aware of in order to maximize your deduction:

- In counting days for this calculation, include the days you depart and return to the United States as days outside the United States.

- Transportation days to and from a business destination generally count as business days as long as you take a direct route to the business destination and do not stop first for non-business activities.

- While at your destination, if your presence is required at a particular place for a business purpose, then you can count that day as a business day even if you spend most of the day on non-business activities.

- A business day is one where the principal activity during working hours is the pursuit of your trade of your business. Also included are holidays, weekends, and any other standby days between business days.

Primarily for Personal Reasons

Finally, if you take a trip outside of the United States that is primarily for personal reasons, the entire cost of the trip is a nondeductible personal expense. However, if you attend a seminar or have a business meeting while on the vacation, you can deduct the fees and other direct expenses of the business activity. This rule was written for all the small business owners who are rarely ever able to escape their work. Even when on a personal vacation thousands of miles away, they get calls and emails from the office asking them to remotely manage and put out fires. Well, as frustrating as that is, at least they can deduct any expenses related to the unwanted interruptions.

Conventions

If you can show that your attendance at a convention benefits your business, you can deduct your travel expenses. This requirement applies even if you are appointed or elected as a delegate of an organization. Make sure you keep the agenda or program materials from the convention, as these documents are the best evidence to show that the convention is connected to your business. Avoid conventions that are for investment, political, social, or other purposes unrelated to your business, as you cannot deduct expenses for these events. Finally, you might want to think twice about attending a foreign convention, as the IRS has a four-point reasonableness test to judge deductions for conventions outside the North American area. Be prepared to provide a lot of detail on the purpose of the event and activities, the sponsoring organization, and the residences of active members in the organization, in order to prove that the convention location was reasonable.

Cruise Ships

For those of you with sea legs who prefer to attend a seminar, convention, or similar business meetings on a cruise ship, please be aware that you can only deduct up to $2,000 per year. If that doesn't take the wind out of your sail, the following five rules are sure to do so:

- The convention, seminar, or meeting has to be directly related to your business.

- The cruise ship has to be a vessel registered in the United States.

- All of the cruise ship's ports of call are in the United States or a possession of the United States.

- You have to sign and attach a written statement to your return that details the total days of the trip, number of hours each day devoted to scheduled business activities, and a program of scheduled business activities.

- You also have to attach a written statement signed by an officer of the organization or group sponsoring the meeting, including a schedule for each day and the number of hours you attended the scheduled business activities.

Whether you actually read all the rules or just skimmed them after the first few, I am guessing by now you are just going to stick with the seminars and conventions on dry land.

Chapter 14

MEALS AND ENTERTAINMENT EXPENSES

I t may be that there is no such thing as a free lunch, but a lunch where Uncle Sam picks up part of the tab is not that bad—especially when that lunch helps you seal an important business deal. While most small business owners are familiar with the meals and entertainment deduction and the 50 percent limitation rule, few understand the actual IRS rules and recordkeeping requirements. In addition, many small business owners are unaware of the other types of entertainment that can be deducted and strategies that can be used to maximize expenses. Instead of using the rules to their advantage and documenting expenses properly, far too many small business owners recklessly deduct any meal they feel is business related and take the gamble that they will not be audited.

This chapter not only explains what entertainment can be deducted, what limits apply, and how much can be deducted, but also how to document your expenses so that they can withstand an IRS audit. With an understanding of the rules and exceptions covered in this chapter, you will be able to maximize your entertainment expenses and avoid missing out on important tax savings.

WHAT ENTERTAINMENT CAN BE DEDUCTED?

The IRS gives us a very broad definition to work with when it comes to entertainment. Like other deductions, the IRS requires that the entertainment be business-related and ordinary and necessary for your business. The expenses also cannot be lavish or extravagant, so keep it within reason relative to your business and the facts and circumstances. Basically, if you cannot explain the business purpose of the deduction in a simple statement with a straight face, you may need to reevaluate whether the expense should be deducted.

As to the type of entertainment, the IRS leaves it open to any activities that provide entertainment, amusement, and recreation. For the most part, the type of entertainment deduction largely depends on your type of business and your circumstances, but the IRS also provides two tests to use in determining if you can deduct specific entertainment expenses.

TWO TESTS OF DEDUCTIBILITY

To deduct an entertainment expense, it must pass one of the two tests developed by the IRS. The first test, the *directly-related* test, is a strict test for entertainment that is directly combined with business. If your entertainment expense does not qualify under the first test, it may qualify under the *associated* test, which is much more flexible test as it allows for entertainment that does not happen at the same time as the business discussion.

The Directly-Related Test

To pass this test, you must show that the main purpose of the combined business and entertainment was the active conduct of business. In other words, the entertainment should be secondary to the business that is taking place during the entertainment. You must also be able to show that you were engaged in business during the entertainment, and that you had more than a general expectation of getting income or some other specific business benefit in the future from the business meeting.

Under this rule, you should closely examine the reasons for carrying out business during the entertainment. Did the entertainment facilitate the business discussion or meeting? Was it necessary in order to get a chance to have a business discussion? If so, document these facts as they offer important proof that the entertainment passes this test. Remember, business has to be the primary purpose. If you have a short business discussion at the very end of a meal, you will likely not pass this test.

The directly-related test rules out certain types of entertainment that, by their nature, do not allow for the active conduct of business because of the substantial distractions the activities create. Nightclubs, sporting events, and movie theaters simply do not allow you the opportunity to carry out active business. Likewise, social gatherings and parties also provide similar distractions that would hinder active business. Finally, hunting and fishing trips generally do not pass this test, so your quail-hunting trip in Texas will have to pass the associated test.

As with all IRS rules, there are exceptions to the directly-related test. If the entertainment takes place in what the IRS calls a "clear business setting", and it is for your business, then it is considered directly-related and passes the test. This would include entertainment at a business event like a tradeshow or convention, or a publicity event where those being entertained do not have any personal or social relationships with you, and you are just trying to get business publicity.

Also, any meals or entertainment provided at meetings at your business location would likely fall under this exception and pass the test.

The Associated Test

For entertainment that does not pass the directly-related test, there is still hope for deductibility using the associated test. To pass this test, you must show the IRS that the entertainment is:

- associated with the active conduct of your business, and
- directly before or after a **substantial** business discussion.

Translated, this means that there must be a clear business purpose to show that it is associated with your business, and you must be able to show that you actively engaged in a meeting, discussion, negotiation, or some other type of business transaction at some time before or after the entertainment. To prove the business discussion was substantial, the purpose of the meeting should be to get income or some other future business benefit. This will depend on the facts of the case, but there is no specified length of time that the business discussion has to be, and the IRS is not going to compare the length of time of the entertainment to the business discussion. As long as the business discussion is substantial in relation to the meal or entertainment, this test should be fairly easy to pass.

The flexibility that this test offers is that the business discussion and the meal or entertainment do not have to be at the same time or even on the same day. In fact, business does not even need to be discussed during the entertainment portion. Just make sure you document the facts and the business discussion—especially if it is on a different day than the entertainment.

This test would allow you to deduct entertainment expenses for activities that have substantial distractions that do not allow for the active conduct of business that we discussed earlier. For example, a sporting event expense could be deductible if you had a substantial business discussion before or after the game. Also, that quail-hunting trip in Texas could now be deductible under this test given the right circumstances. Just be careful not to accidentally shoot your client or customer in the process!

If your entertainment cost does not pass this test, it is likely non-deductible unless you can make arrangements so that it does pass one of the tests. In fact, now that you understand the IRS rules, all of your planned business entertainment costs should pass one of the two tests.

LIMITATIONS ON MEALS AND ENTERTAINMENT

As a small business owner, you are likely well aware of the bad news when it comes to deductibility of meals and entertainment expenses. For tax purposes, the IRS gives your meals and entertainment expense amount a sizable haircut by only allowing you to deduct 50 percent of the expense as a tax deduction unless an exception applies. For example, if you have $4,000 in total meals and entertainment expense for the year, only $2,000 is deductible for tax purposes and the other $2,000 becomes a non-deductible expense.

As mentioned in chapter 13 when discussing the meals deduction when traveling away from home, transportation workers subject to the "hours of service" limits can deduct 80 percent of meals and entertainment expenses incurred while subject to the limits. It is important to note that this would only include the meals incurred while subject to the limits, which would mean you would generally be traveling away from home. If the owner of a trucking company has a business meal in town while not driving or subject to the hour limits, the 50 percent limit would apply.

Exceptions to the 50 Percent Limit

Make sure you are not limiting your entertainment deductions unnecessarily. There are a variety of circumstances that qualify for exception from the 50 percent limit, which many small business owners unfortunately miss or do not properly split out in their accounting records.

- **Advertising**—if food is provided to the general public in an attempt to promote the business or goodwill, the cost of the food is not subject to the 50 percent limit.

- **Employee Party**—generally entertainment expenses for employee parties and events are fully deductible as long as the event is primarily for the employees and not just the owners, family members of the owners, or highly compensated employees.

- **Charitable Sports Event**—if you purchase tickets for a charitable sports event, the 50 percent limit does not apply if the event's main purpose is the benefit of a qualified charitable organization, the entire net proceeds go to charity, and the event uses volunteers to perform substantially all the work.

- **Gifted meals**—if you pay for a meal for a client, customer, or a business associate and you are not present at the meal, you can treat it as a gift rather than meals and entertainment expense. The expense would not be subject to the 50 percent limit, but it would be subject to the $25 gift limit. As long as it is not a four-course meal at an expensive restaurant, the gifting limit can end up giving you a higher deduction.

- **Meals and snacks provided at employer premises**—if provided to more than half the employees and for the employer's convenience, meals provided at meetings or as a means of enticement for working late or over the weekend are not subject to the 50 percent limit. Also, snacks, coffee, soft drinks and other essentials provided in the office are fully deductible.

- **Meals reimbursed by a customer**—if you are a subcontractor that is reimbursed for meals by a customer, the reimbursed meals are not subject to the 50 percent limit. The total cost is deductible and is offset against the reimbursement from the customer.

HOW MUCH CAN I DEDUCT?

One of the biggest issues with meals and entertainment—especially with regard to meals and entertainment costs for meetings between owners of a business—is the question of how much can be deducted without creating red flags that would draw the attention of the IRS. This stems from the fact that every type of business is different and each requires a different level of entertainment costs, which is why the IRS provides detailed tests for determining what is deductible, but remains fairly silent on how much can be deducted. Much of what we have to go on as tax professionals is based on court cases that addressed this specific issue, but the best guide to use is often a simple reasonableness test.

Is It Reasonable?

While it may seem like common sense, a quick, self-assessed reasonableness test is key to avoiding problems with the IRS with regard to entertainment expenses. The most common method that can be used on a regular basis is to calculate your total entertainment expenses as a percentage of gross receipts. Your accounting software should allow you do this with a few clicks as well as let you compare the meals and entertainment balance to other types of expense categories. There is no hard and fast percentage or amount to stay under as every industry is different, but if your total meals and entertainment expense is over 1 percent of gross receipts and larger than many of the other expense categories, you will want to make sure that you have good documentation and that the business purpose for the entertainment expenses is clear. For more information on how the IRS approaches entertainment expenses in audits for your specific industry, review the Audit Technique Guide for your industry on the IRS website (www.irs.gov).

In addition to looking at the big picture, you should also review the reasonableness of each entertainment expense as you incur them. This is not as important in a business with multiple, unrelated owners, as they typically have managing owners who judge the reasonableness of an entertainment expense when they decide whether or not to reimburse it, whereas a one-owner businesses lacks such internal review. If you do not have anyone in your business to whom you have to justify your entertainment expenses, you have to be cautious and consider what a reasonable person would do if they had to submit the expense on a reimbursement request. If you can easily defend an entertainment expense, then reasonableness should not be a problem—especially if the expense passes one of the two tests and is ordinary and necessary for your industry.

Frequency of Entertainment Expenses
In addition to reasonableness, small business owners need to look at the frequency of their entertainment expenses. If the expense is for a meal or other type of entertainment with a client, customer, or other unrelated business associate, this is not as much of an issue as the frequency would largely depend on what is needed to make the sale or secure a future business benefit. However, when it is a meal expense for a business discussion or meeting between the owners of a business or

someone you are related to, frequency is a very important consideration. After all, the point of a business meal or other type of entertainment is that it provides a casual environment where you can get to know someone and ease into a business discussion or sales presentation—especially in cases where a direct approach would not have worked.

Based on court cases addressing this issue, daily lunches between business owners are not deductible (*Moss v. Commissioner* 758 F.2d 211 – 7th Cir. 1985) while a monthly lunch would probably be deductible (*Wells v. Commissioner*, 1977-419, aff'd without opinion, 625 F.2d 868 – 9th Cir. 1980). Depending on the facts and circumstances, somewhere in-between daily and monthly would probably work for business meals between business owners. The same would probably be true for business meals between business owners and employees. If the owners or employees are married, family members, or related in some way, you have to be cautious and make sure the business purpose is very clear. For example, if it is inconvenient to have a meeting with the owners at the office, an occasional management meeting at a restaurant could be justified, but frequent management meetings at a restaurant would be harder to defend if there is a conference room available where management could discuss sensitive matters freely.

PERSONAL VS. BUSINESS ENTERTAINMENT

Entertainment expenses that fail the directly-related and associated tests are clearly non-deductible personal costs, but what about events where both business and non-business individuals are entertained? After all, real life situations are never as black and white as the IRS rules and examples. In business, you are going to have some business meetings where non-business individuals are present—whether they are non-owner spouses and dependents or just other individuals who are present with the business individuals. In these situations, you can only deduct the business portion.

If the costs cannot be separated, you can calculate the business portion on a pro rata basis. However, if it is an employee party or event, you do not have to split out the costs if the employees are allowed to bring a spouse or significant other, as it is a special case where all the costs are fully deductible.

If a small business owner dines alone while not traveling away from home, the meals are generally non-deductible personal costs. Refer to chapter 13 to review what it means to travel away from home, but generally most short day trips, even if outside your tax home, do not qualify as traveling away from home, so be careful not to deduct these personal costs if you eat alone. An exception to this rule would be a networking event where the sole business purpose of attending is to network and find new clients or customers. These networking events typically involve dinner and drinks and most participants come alone.

Country Clubs and Golf and Athletic Clubs

Membership dues and initiation fees for country clubs, golf and athletic clubs, sailing clubs, or any other type of social clubs are generally not deductible. These clubs are usually organized for pleasure, recreation, or social purposes and are personal in nature. However, if you have a business meal at the club or follow up a game of golf with a substantial business meeting, these expenses can be deducted.

If you pay for membership dues and initiation fees through a business, make sure it is listed as non-deductible expense or a draw in the case of a pass-through entity like an LLC or S corporation.

Entertainment Expense Recordkeeping

You can follow every rule on entertainment from Publication 463, but if you fail to substantiate your expenses, they are not going to hold up in audit. Some small business owners who are aware of the IRS rule about not needing to keep receipts on expenses under $75 take that to mean that entertainment expenses under $75 do not need any documentation support at all. Unfortunately, this is a common misunderstanding that can get business owners in trouble and in an audit situation.

While you may not have to keep receipts under $75, you are still required to document the details of each meal and entertainment expense. The IRS wants record of:

- who was entertained,
- where the entertainment took place,
- what the business purpose was, and
- when it took place.

This information cannot be vague statements if you want to pass IRS scrutiny. It should be detailed enough to describe the business discussion or meeting, and any result from the meeting—even if it is just an expected future benefit for your business. If you keep good documentation and lots of it, usually the auditors will not spend much time going through the detail of your expense reports.

With how busy most small business owners are these days, recordkeeping is a painful task that is hard to find time for. However, with the software and smartphone apps that are available these days, it is just a matter of finding a system that works best for you. Most of us enter our appointments in Outlook or a similar program, so why not input the details of a business meal right there in the software? It is fairly painless if you record the information right when it happens, but if you wait until a few months after the business meal, you are not going to remember, so make it a priority to stay current. Tax savings are at risk if you have poor records.

Chapter 15

RETIREMENT PLANS

In today's recessionary economy, all the doom and gloom in the news makes it easy for a new small business owner to procrastinate setting up and contributing to a retirement plan. In fact, it is quite understandable that people are currently more concerned about paying down debt and building up emergency funds than saving for retirement, and, honestly, they should be if debt or cash flow is an issue. However, if you have sufficient cash flow and you have not set up a retirement plan for your business, you are not only missing out on substantial tax deductions, but also important retirement planning opportunities.

If you already have a retirement plan in place, this chapter can serve as reference tool and a refresher on the different plans available, as it is important to evaluate your plan periodically to make sure it is still meeting your needs. As your business grows or your retirement needs change, often you can grow out of a plan, so make sure you have a good financial planner that checks in with you on a regular basis. Unfortunately, there are too many financial planners out there looking for a quick commission and then simply "set and forget" your account. If the only communication you get from your planner is a newsletter, you may want to find someone new.

This chapter provides a brief overview of the qualified retirement plans available to small businesses and compares the limits and tax considerations for each plan. This is not an in-depth study, as it is only intended to provide the information you need to know as a small business owner. Your tax professional and financial planner can help you with all the boring details not covered in this chapter and make sure your plan stays in compliance.

WHY SET UP A RETIREMENT PLAN?

Most of us know we should save more for retirement. Any lack of action and follow-through is not from a deficiency of information or tax incentives, but simply the fact that it is much more exciting to spend money on a vacation or gadgets than sock it away long-term for retirement. I could go on and on about the fact that Social Security benefits will not be enough (or there at all) and how investing earlier in life will provide exponential growth and accumulation; but the decision to set up and contribute to a retirement plan needs to come from the correct motivation and you need to have the resources available to commit long-term.

The current tax rules offer great incentive for a small business owner to contribute to retirement. It is by no means a dollar-for-dollar incentive, but if it coincides with your retirement savings goals and cash flow situation, it can result in substantial savings that you would be foolish to not take advantage of. If that is not enough, there is also a tax credit available for qualified businesses that start new retirement plans, which is discussed at the end of this chapter, so the tax incentives are many. That being said, you should not start a retirement plan for the tax savings alone. Some small business owners—especially those that find out they have a large, unexpected tax liability near the return due date—start a retirement plan quickly to reduce their tax bill. While there is nothing wrong with using a retirement plan to reduce your tax liability, problems can result if you do not spend enough time on cash flow and retirement planning and simply pick whatever plan is available at the time. This type of eleventh hour retirement contribution may work in the short-term, but often it can cause problems several years down the road if there is a cash flow problem for the business owner or the retirement plan selected was not the best for the business. My advice—plan ahead, carefully budget your cash flow, and spend time with a financial planner to make sure you have a retirement plan that meets your needs.

UNDERSTANDING THE BASICS OF RETIREMENT PLANS

Learning all the detailed rules of each type of retirement plan can be very confusing, and as a small business owner you really do not need to know everything as long as you have a good tax professional and financial planner. However, you should understand the basics and the underlying principles involved.

Defined Contribution vs. Defined Benefit

First off, there are two types of qualified retirement plans available:

- Defined contribution plans
- Defined benefit pension plans

The path you take defines either your contribution amount or your retirement benefit. The most common retirement plans used in small businesses are defined contribution plans, and there are many different varieties available that offer different annual tax-deductible contribution amounts. Contributions to these plans are discretionary, which is an important advantage as you can adjust for changes in cash flow. This is not the case with defined benefit pension plans, which have mandatory annual contributions. They are also complicated and expensive as compared to defined contribution plans, so even though they offer the largest annual contributions, most small business owners use defined contribution plans.

What Retirement Plans Are Available?

There are a variety of qualified retirement plans available. Several of the plans are suited for specific business entities with specific circumstances, while others like the SIMPLE IRA and 401k are available to a broad range of small businesses. Below is a brief overview of each type of plan, which will be discussed in more detail later in this chapter.

- **Simplified Employee Pension Plans (SEPs)**— these plans are easy to set up and work best for self-employed individuals and companies with few employees. The plan can become very costly as more employees become eligible.

- **Solo 401k (Individual 401k)**—this is a great plan for profitable, self-employed individuals and businesses with no full-time employees other than the owner and spouse. Contribution limits are sizable—especially if a spouse is involved with the business.

- **SIMPLE IRAs**—rightly-named, the SIMPLE IRA is a simplified, low-cost retirement plan for businesses that includes employee contributions and employer matching. Despite the simplicity, the contribution limits can be restrictive, as they are lower than those available under a 401k plan.

- **401k plans**—as the most common qualified retirement plan used by large and small companies, the 401k offers higher contribution limits and employer matching. However, they are more complex and have higher administration costs.

- **Profit Sharing Plan (PSPs)**—when combined with a 401k plan, a profit sharing plan is a great benefit to both the owners and the rank-and-file employees. It basically allows you to reach the contribution limits of the SEP using a 401k. Contributions are discretionary, but the rules and calculations involved can be very complex, so expect high administration costs.

- **Defined Benefit Plan (DBPs)**—as mentioned earlier, even though these plans offer high annual contribution limits, they are very complex and costly. However, some businesses have the right mix of circumstances that make these plans a good fit, so talk to your financial planner.

THE INDIVIDUAL RETIREMENT ACCOUNT (IRA) ALTERNATIVE

Before we get into the details of each type of retirement plan, and before you get too excited and call your financial planner, you should take an honest look at how much you are looking to contribute and consider a low-cost alternative to setting up a retirement plan. If you are a self-employed individual with a fairly small business, often a traditional IRA account can meet your retirement planning needs and provide you with adequate tax savings. In 2012, an individual with earned income can contribute $5,000 ($6,000 if over fifty years old by year-end), and for some micro-businesses and start-ups, this amount may be sufficient.

Your financial planner will likely not recommend this low-cost option as they naturally get very low commissions from IRA accounts. Plus, the IRA is rather boring and as a professional, you want to present exciting ideas with big tax savings. However, sometimes tax and financial planning professionals overcomplicate life for sole proprietors and micro-businesses. I have seen this happen many times in my career and it is frustrating as any tax benefits are often erased by investment and tax preparation fees. In some cases, the problem lies with the business owner, as sometimes we all give in to the "bigger is better" sales pitch, but as professionals we should be helping you choose the option that is best suited for you and your business, even if that option ends up being a common sense solution like the IRA.

Pairing Up Your IRA for Additional Tax Savings

If the low limit of the IRA does not work for you and you still want a simple, low-cost solution, consider using the IRA in combination with other types of non-retirement savings plan like the HSA or an education savings plan for your children. The combination of the annual amounts contributed to these plans may fit your planning needs. If you are fairly healthy, amounts not spent on medical expenses and held in an HSA plan are essentially just like the funds in your IRA account, so you could consider the combined contributions to your IRA and HSA plans as your overall "retirement" contribution.

The Roth IRA Option

Instead of contributing to a traditional IRA account, you can contribute a Roth IRA. However, keep in mind that you do not receive a current year tax deduction, and that the tax-free benefit is received when you take the distribution in retirement. Which option is better largely depends on your circumstances and what your income will look like in retirement.

Overall, the IRA alternative to an actual retirement plan is worth looking into—especially if you are young, but as your business grows and you get closer to retirement, an actual retirement plan becomes a necessity.

QUALIFIED PLAN CONTRIBUTION
LIMITS AND TAX CONSIDERATIONS

Now that you have a basic understanding of all the qualified retirement plans available, you are ready to learn the contribution limits and tax considerations for each plan. Each of the following plans is considered a *qualified* plan, which means they have to meet strict requirements under federal law. As much as I encourage the do-it-yourself attitude among informed small business owners, this is not an area to try and handle on your own. Find a good financial planner, broker, or other investment advisor that will help you avoid problems and stay compliant with all the federal laws pertaining to your plan.

SIMPLIFIED EMPLOYEE PENSION PLANS (SEPs)

Also called the SEP IRA, this plan is a flexible option for self-employed individuals and small corporations with few or no employees. For 2012, the maximum annual contribution is the lesser of:

- $50,000, or

- 25 percent of the participant's taxable compensation (20 percent of self-employment income if self-employed).

The best part about the SEP is that it is a good "eleventh hour" option for small business owners who procrastinate as you can set up and contribute to a SEP as late as the due date of the tax return plus extensions. Keep in mind; you actually have to file an extension timely to get the additional time. Set up of a SEP is fairly painless, and if you do not have employees the calculation if simple.

If you have employees, you have to contribute the same percentage to those employees that are eligible, which can be very costly. Either that or you have to limit your contribution to a lower percentage amount, which will then lower the employee contribution. However, employees are not eligible until they have:

- three years of service (out of the last five years),
- are twenty-one years or older, and
- have earned at least $450 in compensation for the year.

These rules should give you some flexibility for a few years after initially hiring employees; however, the same eligibility rules can prevent a spouse from qualifying for a contribution, so make sure you consider all the possible outcomes before having your SEP plan written up.

The SEP plan does not work as well for S corporation shareholders who pay themselves a small wage or an LLC member with a small amount of self-employment income. This is due to the fact that the contribution is based on wages or income subject to self-employment tax. In these cases, the Solo 401k or Simple IRA plans should be considered.

Solo 401k (Individual 401k)

If you are feeling limited by the SEP plan, the Solo 401k plan is a great solution as long as you qualify. The plan is available to self-employed individuals and business owners with no full time W-2 employees other than themselves or a spouse.

The maximum annual contribution for 2012 is $50,000 ($55,500 if the participant is fifty years or older). If you have a very profitable business that your spouse works for, you could have a combined annual contribution of $100k or $111k if you are both over the age of fifty. Now, you may notice that the maximum contribution limit for those under age fifty is the same as the SEP limit; however, this does not mean they provide the same retirement benefits and tax deductions. The

Solo 401k calculation is very different than the SEP, and less income is needed under the Solo 401k to reach that maximum limit, so in most circumstances the Solo 401k is going the better option.

The maximum Solo 401k contribution is composed of the following:

- the 401(k) deferral of $17,000,

- the 401(k) catch-up deferral of $5,500 (if age fifty or older), and

- the profit sharing contribution of up to $33,000.

The profit sharing contribution portion is calculated just like the SEP contribution, so it is 25 percent of the participant's taxable wages, or 20 percent of self-employment income if self-employed. Without the deferral portion, the SEP and Solo 401k are virtually identical, but because you can defer 100 percent of your compensation or self-employment income up to the deferral limits, the Solo 401k provides a much larger contribution with less income than the SEP.

The only drawback of the Solo 401k is that you can outgrow the plan if your business grows and full-time employees are required. Generally, you can exclude employees under twenty-one, employees with less than one year of service, those who work less than 1000 hours per year, and certain union and nonresident alien employees. The one-year service requirement can buy you some time; however, you would need to eventually switch to a regular 401k plan when you can no longer exclude your employees. At that point, if you wanted to continue making profit sharing contributions, the contribution that would be required for the employees could be costly, so the benefits are definitely not as good as with the Solo 401k.

Another drawback of the Solo 401k is the administration cost. The plan is more costly to set up and maintain than the SEP and SIMPLE IRA, and after the assets in the plan exceed

$100k, the IRS requires an annual Form 5500 filing. However, generally these costs are well worth the additional contributions that the Solo 401k can provide.

SIMPLE IRAs

If you want to avoid the large administration costs of a 401k and do not need the higher contribution limits, the SIMPLE IRA is an easy, low-cost solution. The SIMPLE IRA, short for *Saving Incentive Match For Employees*, also works well if you have a number of full-time employees that would make you ineligible for the Solo 401k or make the SEP plan far too costly.

For 2012, the maximum annual deferral contribution for a business owner or employee is $11,500 ($14,000 if age fifty or older). This deferral contribution is optional to owners and employees, but there is also a mandatory employer match due annually by the employer's tax filing deadline (including extensions). The employer match can be made one of two ways:

- A 3 percent employer match paid to employees who elected to make a deferral contribution from their salary. The match is a dollar for dollar contribution of their deferral up to 3 percent of their salary. For highly compensated employees, the maximum limit would be $11,500 or $14,000 if age fifty or older. Under this method, an employer can reduce the employer match to 1 percent of each participating employee's compensation for any two years in a five-year period.

- A 2 percent match of employee compensation (up to $4,900 in 2012) for all eligible employees regardless of whether they elected to make a deferral contribution or not.

Does this plan still sound simple? Well, admittedly the employer match can be confusing; however, if you stick with the 3 percent match each year, it can get easier to understand and calculate. Ask your tax professional to calculate your match at year-end or when they prepare your tax return. You cannot depend on your investment advisor or financial planner to do this as SIMPLE IRA accounts are "set and forget" accounts, and they rarely inquire if they do not receive an employer contribution.

The drawback of the SIMPLE IRA is obviously the lower contribution limits, and most financial planners do not suggest the plan for this reason. I get their point, but many businesses do not need all the cost and complication that comes with the much more formal 401k. Plus, if your spouse is involved with the business and you are both over fifty, you can sock away $28,000 per year, which should be sufficient for many retirement plans. Combine that with the maximum HSA contribution ($6,250 for 2012, $7,250 if over age fifty) each year, and as long as your medical expenses are fairly low, that gives you a fairly large retirement contribution each year.

The 401k

The 401k is the retirement plan that you are likely most familiar with if you spent any time at all as an employee. Most companies offer the plan because it provides high contribution limits and a solid, standardized employee benefit. More importantly, 401k plans allow participants to designate a portion of their deferral as a Roth contribution, which provides flexibility that the other qualified plans simply cannot offer.

The maximum annual contribution limit for 2012 is $17,000 ($22,500 if you are age fifty or older). Keep in mind; this is only the employee deferral portion. If you have a profit sharing plan, the overall limit of employee deferral and employer contribution is much higher, which will be discussed in the next section.

Generally, a 401k plan must be open to employees that are twenty-one years of age or older and have completed a year of service Employer matching is fairly flexible and can be set up in a number of different ways. The most common match is 50 percent of the employee contribution up to 6 percent of their wages. Dollar for dollar matches of up to 5 percent of wages are also fairly common. Most plans are set up as "pay to play" plans where only employees who make contributions receive a match.

The 401k plan also offers participants the ability to take loans on the vested account balance (generally up to 50 percent of the balance with a maximum of $50,000). The problem is if you use this option as the owner, you also have to allow loans for employees, which means additional administration costs and headaches. My advice is to not allow loans in your 401k plan at all. Investment advisors were strongly promoting this feature before the recession as a means to invest in real estate, and as you can imagine, this created disaster for some business owners. Don't get me wrong; some owners use 401k loans responsibly, but most of the time it far better to leave retirement contributions untouched until retirement.

There are a variety of plan types that simplify the rules and testing requirements, so make sure you meet with your financial planner and tax professional to find the right fit for your business. If you use one of the larger payroll services, often they offer all-in-one 401k solutions that automatically integrate with your payroll processing service; however, that integration can be more costly depending on your circumstances.

PROFIT SHARING PLAN (PSPs)

If you have a profitable business and want to contribute more to your retirement while also offering profit sharing benefits to employees, a profit sharing plan is a great companion to a 401k plan. It is costly and involves complicated calculations that will have to be completed by an attorney or a specialist; however, often the benefits to the business owners are well worth the cost.

A profit sharing plan is similar to the profit sharing component of the Solo 401k that we have already discussed. The only difference is that it is much more complicated with qualifying employees, and you will likely have to contribute a sizable amount to employees if you want to maximize your benefit.

For 2012, the maximum annual employer contribution under a profit sharing plan is $33,000, which means the overall 401k contribution could be as much as $50,000 ($55,500 if over age fifty).

DEFINED BENEFIT PLAN (DBPs)

If you have a stable, profitable business with few or no employees other than yourself, and you are looking to contribute larger amounts for retirement than the defined contribution plans allow, then a defined benefit plan may work well for you. This is especially true if you are age fifty or older and trying to catch up on your retirement funding.

Basically, a DBP is set up to provide a specific annual retirement payment, beginning at retirement age, that can be a flat monthly amount, a fixed percentage of income, or a specific formula based on years of service. Once you decide on the retirement promise, you have to hire an actuary to compute the annual contributions, which can be costly. The contributions are deductible and can be made as late as the due date of the tax return, including extensions, for the year of deduction.

For 2012, the annual contribution limit is $200,000, which should allow most small business owners to catch up on retirement funding rather quickly.

The main disadvantages to using a DBP are mandatory contributions, costly administration and professional assistance costs, and the fact that they can be very costly if you hire any employees twenty-one years or older who work 1,000 hours or more during any twelve-month period.

OTHER OPTIONS FOR HIGH-INCOME BUSINESS OWNERS

If you have a very profitable business and qualified plans do not provide enough for your retirement, there are non-qualified plans available that are much less restrictive, and when combined with a qualified plan, they can help you build a larger retirement nest egg.

The three most common non-qualified plans are Split-Dollar Insurance plans, Executive Bonus plans, and Deferred Compensation plans. Each of these plans meet different needs and have different requirements, so you will definitely need an experienced financial planner who is willing to look at your entire financial picture—both business and personal—to find a solution that will work best for you.

Some of the options will require you to make changes to the structure of your business, so make sure your tax professional and financial planner are working together on establishing your non-qualified plan. Some tax professionals also offer financial planning services, and while there is nothing wrong with this, when it comes to non-qualified plans it is better to engage an independent specialist.

HOW DO I SETUP A RETIREMENT PLAN?

As I mentioned earlier, do not attempt to setup a retirement plan on your own! It is not a do-it-yourself project and you will only create problems for yourself in the long-term. Do some shopping around to get an idea of the different pricing structures available, and then make sure you follow through and engage a good financial planner, stock broker, or investment advisor that will look at your entire financial picture and work with your tax professional to find a plan that will work best for you and your business. Make sure you plan ahead and meet with your financial planner well in advance of the retirement plan start date. Some plans have to be set up by specific deadlines, so procrastination may limit your options.

TAX CREDIT FOR STARTING A NEW PLAN

If you are worried about the cost of setting up a new retirement plan, Uncle Sam will actually pay up to $1,500 of your costs of setting up the plan over the first three years. The credit is equal to 50 percent of the first $1,000 in administrative and retirement-education expenses for each of the three years. As long as you have at least one non-owner, non-highly compensated employee eligible to participate, and it is a newly established plan, then generally you will be eligible for the credit.

Large employers who employ more than 100 employees who received compensation in excess of $5,000 are not eligible. Also, if you are part of an affiliated service group or controlled by a larger employer, you will likely not be eligible for the credit. Check with your tax professional to see if you qualify.

Chapter 16

OFFICE IN HOME DEDUCTION

For home-based businesses, the office in home deduction is often very important, as it is one of the major costs of doing business. Even if the office in home deduction itself is not that significant, the benefit a home office can provide for maximizing vehicle expenses by reducing personal commuting miles is crucial, which is discussed in chapter 12. If you have a main office outside of the home, you should still be aware of the office in home rules, as there are some exceptions that may allow you a deduction.

In this chapter we will walk through the requirements and exceptions of the office in home rules and look at how the deduction can be taken for the owner of a corporation. We will also discuss calculation of the deduction and the tax traps that can result if you take depreciation on your home.

WHAT QUALIFIES AS AN OFFICE IN HOME?

For a space in a home to qualify for the office in home deduction, it must be used exclusively and regularly for a trade or business. In addition, it must be the principal place of business or qualify for one of the exceptions available to those with multiple business locations.

If you are an employee, there are additional rules to consider, which we will discuss later in this chapter, but the office in home deduction is definitely easier for sole proprietorships to claim. For other business entities, there are additional steps and different approaches available, but they all build on the same foundational rules.

Exclusive Use Requirement

What does it mean to use a space exclusively for business? Well, in this case the IRS is fairly literal, and other than de minimis personal use, you have to have a room or separate, identifiable space that is used wholly for business. For the most part, it is an uncompromising rule in which any combined personal and business use disqualifies the space for the office in home deduction. This may not seem realistic or even fair, but the IRS is rarely either, so it is best to learn the rules and exceptions first and then arrange your business affairs around the rules. You will fair much better in an audit than the business owner who simply tries to interpret or fit IRS rules around their circumstances.

De Minimis Personal Use

What does de minimis personal use mean? Well, it is not necessarily the same as minimal personal use, as personal use for the most part disqualifies a room or space. Based on court cases, de minimis personal use has more to do with walking through rooms or spaces for both business and personal use. This is important in a small home where a bathroom or garage may only be accessible by walking through the business office. Most tax professionals would agree that this type of use would not disqualify the space for the office in home deduction, but any personal use beyond walking through the room or space would likely put you at risk of disqualification in an audit.

Partial Room Use

If you do not use an entire room, make sure the space used for business is a separate, identifiable space. This does not mean that you have to have a permanent partition to mark off the space, but there should be some sort of separation from the rest of the room that easily indentifies it as an office. If you use multiple rooms, again make sure that each room is used exclusively for business.

Exceptions to Exclusive Use

There are two exceptions to the exclusive use rule available to those who use part of their home for storage of inventory or a daycare facility. The exceptions are detailed, so make sure you meet all the requirements of the exception.

Storage of Inventory

If you use part of your home for the storage of inventory or product samples, you can use the office in home deduction without meeting the exclusive use test. However, you must meet all of the following tests:

- you must be in the business of selling products at wholesale or retail,

- you must actually keep the inventory or product samples used in the business in your home,

- your home must be the only fixed location of your business,

- the storage space must be used on a regular basis, and

- the space must be a separately identifiable space suitable for storage.

Daycare Facility

If you use part of your home for a daycare facility, you can use the office in home deduction even if you use the same space for non-business purposes, but you must meet the following requirements:

- you must be in business of providing daycare for either children, persons sixty-five or older, or persons who are physically or mentally unable to care for themselves, and

- you must have a license, certification, or other registration issued by the state that allows you to operate as a daycare center or a family or group daycare home.

Daycare facilities also have to use a more complicated method of calculation for the office in home deduction that factors in the hours in which the space is used for business purposes. For more details on this calculation, refer to Publication 587.

Regular Use Requirement

In addition to exclusive business use, an office in home must also be used regularly for business. This means that you use it on a consistent basis for business activities and not just incidental or occasional use.

Even though this is a clear-cut rule as compared to the exclusive use test, you do have to consider your business and the industry it is in when applying this rule. What may be incidental and occasional for one industry may actually be substantial and frequent for another, so you have to apply the facts and circumstances. For example, regular use of an office in home for a bean counter like myself would likely mean using it every business day, but for a contractor that spends significant time at worksites, a few afternoons a week might be completely adequate. Nonetheless, more time spent working in the home office on a regular basis is always going to look better to the IRS, so try to arrange your schedule to best protect your deduction.

Documenting Regular Office Use

Now you may feel that you have this requirement taken care of with no problem, but how will you prove regular use to an IRS auditor? Would you be able to supply some form of documentation proving the regular use of the home office? CPAs like myself often overlook this issue since we bill by time and have been programmed over the years to keep very meticulous records of the time we spend throughout the day. If you are in an industry were it is not as important to keep records of how you spend your time, this may be difficult at first, but you should keep notes on your calendar or a log that proves the home office use. Most business owners keep a calendar in Outlook or on their mobile device, so it should not require too much extra work. I would also suggest making sure you keep all your sent emails on your office computer, fax logs, or any other documents that could prove you were using your home office.

The Principal Place of Business Requirement

Even if a home office is used exclusively and regularly for business, it will not qualify for deduction unless it is also the principal place of business. Either that or the office must meet one of the few exceptions discussed later in this section. For most home-based businesses, this requirement is fairly easy to meet. However, if you have multiple locations, you may have to adjust your business arrangements in order to meet this requirement.

A principal place of business is essentially the place where administrative and management activities are conducted. If you have multiple locations, you can review the relative importance of the activities and the time spent at each location; however, the overriding factor is going to be where the administrative and management activities take place.

Administrative and Management Activities

What does the IRS consider administrative and management activities? Well, according to Publication 587, these activities generally include:

- billing customers, clients, or patients,
- keeping books and records,
- ordering supplies,
- setting up appointments, and
- forwarding orders or writing reports.

Depending on your industry, the activities that would be considered administrative and management may vary slightly, but basically it would be the core tasks required to mange your business.

Generally, your office in home must be the only place where substantial administrative and management activities are conducted, but there are several exceptions to the rule:

- If you hire a service provider to conduct administrative activities on your behalf, the fact that these activities are conducted at a different location does not affect your office in home deduction.
- You can also carry out management and administrative activities in a non-fixed location like a car or hotel room.

- Minimal administrative work that is occasionally done at fixed locations outside of the home is acceptable, which is good considering what can be done from a mobile device these days.

- For work that is not administrative or management-oriented, substantial amounts can be done outside of the home without creating a problem with the office in home deduction.

- Finally, if you have a suitable space outside the home to conduct administrative and management activities, but choose to use your home instead, your office in home can still qualify as the principal place of business.

Exceptions to the Principal Place of Business Rule

There are two exceptions to the principal place of business rule, which were discussed in detail in chapter 12, that allow you to have a qualified office in the home even though it is not the only place where substantial administrative and management activities are conducted. The two exceptions are available if:

- you physically meet with clients, patients or customers in your home office, and it is substantial and integral to your business, or

- your home office is a separate structure from the dwelling unit.

If you meet with clients in your home office, make sure it is with a significant number of clients so that there is no doubt that it is substantial and integral to your business. Also, if you have a separate structure as an office in home, make sure it is large enough to carry out your business activities as the IRS does visit and inspect these structures in audits.

Requirements for Employees

If you are an employee, you have to meet all three requirements discussed above, plus two additional requirements:

- your business use must be for the convenience of the employer, and

- you must not rent any part of your home to your employer and use the rented portion to perform services as an employee.

While these rules have no impact on a self-employed owner of a sole proprietorship, partnership, or LLC, it definitely complicates the deduction for C and S corporations since owners of corporations are employees and not self-employed.

CORPORATIONS AND THE
OFFICE IN HOME DEDUCTION

Even among seasoned tax professionals, you can get a wide variety of solutions for maximizing deductions for a corporate shareholder who uses part of his home exclusively and regularly as the principal place of business for their corporation. Some would have the corporation rent the home office, others would suggest using the employee business expense deduction, and a last group would advocate setting up an accountable plan that reimburses the sharefolder. While all of the options do work, the accountable plan option usually provides the largest deductions with the least amount of tax issues.

The Accountable Plan Method

I stumbled upon this method a few years ago on taxalmanac. org and even though it requires some planning and discipline on the small business owner's part, it is definitely the best method out there for dealing with this problem.

The accountable plan method involves the corporation reimbursing the shareholder employee for a portion of their total home expenses—like mortgage interest, insurance, property tax, and even depreciation—that are applicable to the office in home. The process is very similar to the way a corporation reimburses employees for travel expenses as the shareholder employee would complete an expense report with documentation that substantiates the business expense, and the corporation would pay the reimbursement and deduct the expense for the office space. The shareholder employee would not have any taxable income from the reimbursement; however, the deductions for which they were reimbursed would have to be reduced on the individual tax return. In other words, there is double dipping here—you cannot deduct a portion of mortgage interest and property tax on the corporation and still claim the entire amount of mortgage interest and property tax on the individual return.

Keep in mind, you still have to meet all the requirements for the office in home deduction discussed earlier in this chapter. In addition, you have to meet the requirements for employees, so the use of the home office must be for the convenience of the employer. Also, when you complete the expense report, use IRS Form 8829 as your backup documentation for the report. While you are not actually filing the form, it works well for documentation as you can complete the calculation right on the form.

Rental Methods

If you have been paying attention in this chapter, you may wonder why we would even discuss the option of an employee shareholder renting a home office from a corporation. After all, the second employee requirement for an office in the home is that the employee must not rent any portion of the home to their employer. Well, the IRS allows such a rental as long as only mortgage interest and property tax— which would otherwise be deductible on Schedule A—are the only deductions against the rental income on Schedule E. To see how this works, let's look at how this method applies to each type of corporation.

S Corporation Home Office Rental

When an S corporation rents a home office from a shareholder employee, it appears much like wash on paper, and for the most part it is, except for a minor benefit on the individual tax return side for those that itemize deductions. The corporation would get a deduction for the rent, which flows through to the individual return and basically offsets the rental income recognized on the personal return. The only real change is that a portion of mortgage interest and property tax moves from Schedule A to Schedule E, so you usually end up with a slightly lower adjusted gross income. Otherwise, there really is not much benefit for the shareholder from using the office in home.

C Corporation Home Office Rental

Unlike the S corporation, deductions do not pass-through to the shareholder, so having the corporation rent a home office from a shareholder can result in a wide variety of outcomes, most not as favorable as using the accountable plan method. For example, if your corporation has a net operating loss, the tax benefit from the rent deduction is carried back or forward, but either way you would have a current tax on the individual tax return with no current benefit on the corporate side. Even if the corporation has taxable income, you would have to be careful and watch tax rates on both the corporate and individual side. If taxable income for the corporation is less than $50,000, you are going to get a 15 percent tax benefit on the corporate side, while you would likely pay a much higher rate on the rental income on the personal side. If you are using the rental method with a C corporation, make sure to discuss the issue with your tax professional as the tax impact can vary quite a bit depending on the circumstances.

Employee Business Expense Method

Of the three methods available, this one is probably the worst. I would probably only suggest it for minority shareholders who are employees of a corporation that is not willing to pay rent or reimburse office in home expenses. Reason being is that there is a 2 percent haircut on employee business expenses on Schedule A, and you generally lose a good portion of your deduction. Basically, right off the top you lose 2 percent of your adjusted gross income, and only the amount of the deduction over that amount would be deductible. Granted, if you have other sizable miscellaneous deductions, the impact would not be as great, but for most shareholders, the benefit is very minimal, if anything at all.

Calculating the Office in Home Deduction

While I do not recommend self-preparing a Form 8829 for an office in home deduction, I do think it is important for a small business owner to understand how the calculation works. Not only does it help a business owner better understand their tax return, but it also gives them a better understanding of what information is needed and how the tax professional uses it in the calculation.

The calculation is based primarily on a business percentage, which is calculated by dividing the square footage of the space used exclusively for business into the total square footage of the home. This business percentage is then used to calculate the business portion of the mortgage interest, property taxes, and operating expenses.

As you can see on the sample Form 8829 below, the business use percentage is calculated in Part I, and then the expenses are reported in Part II. Casualty losses, mortgage interest, and property taxes are separated on Form 8829 from operating expenses like insurance, repairs and maintenance, and utilities, and this is a very important distinction in the

Form **8829**	Expenses for Business Use of Your Home	OMB No. 1545-0074
Department of the Treasury Internal Revenue Service (99)	▶ File only with Schedule C (Form 1040). Use a separate Form 8829 for each home you used for business during the year. ▶ See separate instructions.	**20 11** Attachment Sequence No. **176**
Name(s) of proprietor(s)		Your social security number

Part I — Part of Your Home Used for Business

1	Area used regularly and exclusively for business, regularly for daycare, or for storage of inventory or product samples (see instructions)	1	
2	Total area of home	2	
3	Divide line 1 by line 2. Enter the result as a percentage	3	%
	For daycare facilities not used exclusively for business, go to line 4. All others go to line 7.		
4	Multiply days used for daycare during year by hours used per day	4	hr.
5	Total hours available for use during the year (365 days x 24 hours) (see instructions)	5	
6	Divide line 4 by line 5. Enter the result as a decimal amount . . .	6	.
7	Business percentage. For daycare facilities not used exclusively for business, multiply line 6 by line 3 (enter the result as a percentage). All others, enter the amount from line 3 . . . . . ▶	7	%

Part II — Figure Your Allowable Deduction

		(a) Direct expenses	(b) Indirect expenses		
8	Enter the amount from Schedule C, line 29, plus any gain derived from the business use of your home and shown on Schedule D or Form 4797, minus any loss from the trade or business not derived from the business use of your home and shown on Schedule D or Form 4797. See instructions . .			8	
	See instructions for columns (a) and (b) before completing lines 9–21.				
9	Casualty losses (see instructions)	9			
10	Deductible mortgage interest (see instructions)	10			
11	Real estate taxes (see instructions)	11			
12	Add lines 9, 10, and 11	12			
13	Multiply line 12, column (b) by line 7 . . .		13		
14	Add line 12, column (a) and line 13			14	
15	Subtract line 14 from line 8. If zero or less, enter -0-			15	
16	Excess mortgage interest (see instructions) .	16			
17	Insurance	17			
18	Rent	18			
19	Repairs and maintenance	19			
20	Utilities	20			
21	Other expenses (see instructions)	21			
22	Add lines 16 through 21	22			
23	Multiply line 22, column (b) by line 7 . . .		23		
24	Carryover of operating expenses from 2010 Form 8829, line 42 . .		24		
25	Add line 22 column (a), line 23, and line 24			25	
26	Allowable operating expenses. Enter the smaller of line 15 or line 25			26	
27	Limit on excess casualty losses and depreciation. Subtract line 26 from line 15			27	
28	Excess casualty losses (see instructions)	28			
29	Depreciation of your home from line 41 below	29			
30	Carryover of excess casualty losses and depreciation from 2010 Form 8829, line 43	30			
31	Add lines 28 through 30			31	
32	Allowable excess casualty losses and depreciation. Enter the smaller of line 27 or line 31 . .			32	
33	Add lines 14, 26, and 32			33	
34	Casualty loss portion, if any, from lines 14 and 32. Carry amount to Form 4684 (see instructions)			34	
35	Allowable expenses for business use of your home. Subtract line 34 from line 33. Enter here and on Schedule C, line 30. If your home was used for more than one business, see instructions ▶			35	

Part III — Depreciation of Your Home

36	Enter the smaller of your home's adjusted basis or its fair market value (see instructions) . .	36	
37	Value of land included on line 36	37	
38	Basis of building. Subtract line 37 from line 36	38	
39	Business basis of building. Multiply line 38 by line 7	39	
40	Depreciation percentage (see instructions)	40	%
41	Depreciation allowable (see instructions). Multiply line 39 by line 40. Enter here and on line 29 above	41	

Part IV — Carryover of Unallowed Expenses to 2012

42	Operating expenses. Subtract line 26 from line 25. If less than zero, enter -0-	42	
43	Excess casualty losses and depreciation. Subtract line 32 from line 31. If less than zero, enter -0-	43	

For Paperwork Reduction Act Notice, see your tax return instructions.	Cat. No. 13232M	Form **8829** (2011)

event of a loss. If the business does not have net taxable income, the operating expenses are not deductible and have to be carried forward to the next tax year or when the business has net taxable income. However, the mortgage interest, property taxes, and any casualty losses can still be deducted if there is a loss.

Direct expenses would include expenses that are 100 percent business deductions, while indirect expenses are totals for the entire home that need to be multiplied by the business use percentage. The most common direct expense is a repair made to a room that is used exclusively for the office, so make sure you are tracking these expenses separately from repairs made to the rest of the home.

ADVANTAGE TO RENTERS

Since rent is not deductible on the individual return like mortgage interest and property tax, business owners who rent and have an office in home typically receive a much larger tax benefit than those that own a home. However, rent expense is an operating expense on Form 8829, so if you have a taxable loss for the year, you will not receive a current tax benefit and the expense will carry forward.

THE DEPRECIATION TAX TRAP

You may want to avoid depreciating your office in home, as this can have repercussions down the line when you sell your home. Typically, the tax benefit from the depreciation is not very substantial compared to the depreciation recapture that may result. Make sure you discuss this with you tax professional before claiming depreciation on an office in home, as they will be able to look at your circumstances and layout the hypothetical tax impact you could expect.

Chapter 17

TAX BENEFITS FOR EMPLOYERS

I
n 2010, Uncle Sam handed small business employers two important tax benefits that provided tax exemptions and credits for hiring unemployed workers and providing health insurance for employees. Unfortunately, these tax benefits arrived during a time when it seemed like we had a new tax bill released every month, so many small business owners and even some tax professionals missed out on these important benefits that can amount to thousands of dollars in refunds. Luckily, there is still time to make any needed corrections as long as you act quickly.

This chapter provides important information on the HIRE Act incentives and the Small Business Health Care Tax Credit. Both tax benefits are fairly complex; however, as a small business owner, you do not need to fully understand all the rules, so the following is a summary of only the information that you need to be concerned about.

The HIRE Act—Make Sure You Didn't Miss It!

While the Hiring Incentive to Restore Employment Act may be old news for some small business owners at this point, I am finding more and more businesses that were either not aware of the tax benefits from the HIRE Act, or they simply missed reporting an eligible employee. If you hired new employees back in 2010, I would recommend double-checking your records to make sure you received the payroll tax exemptions and tax credits your business is entitled to, which can amount to thousands of dollars. The window of opportunity to make corrections will start closing in 2013, so do not delay in reviewing your records or meeting with your tax professional.

HIRE Act Tax Benefits

President Obama signed the HIRE Act into law on March 18, 2010, which included two related but separate tax benefits:

- **6.2 Percent Payroll Tax Exemption**—if you hired an eligible employee in 2010 between February 3, 2010 and December 31, 2010, your business should have received a holiday from paying the employer share of social security tax on taxable wages paid to the employee. This exemption was claimed on the quarterly 941 filings as a reduction to the employer tax liability, which provides immediate refunds for most businesses.

- **$1,000 Tax Credit**—for each eligible employee that works for your business for at least one year (fifty-two weeks), your business receives a tax credit of $1,000. For calendar year employers, this credit is claimed on the 2011 tax return, but fiscal year filers can claim the credit in the fiscal year in which the eligible employee(s) reached the fifty-two-week mark.

Due to the delay between the reporting of the subsidy and the tax credit, and the fact that the subsidy is handled by your payroll processor and the tax credit is claimed by your tax professional, there is definitely room for error and miscommunication. If you have a good tax professional, they likely checked to make sure you received any benefits due to your business, but it is definitely something you should check with them on.

Which Employees Are Considered Eligible?

To qualify for the tax benefits, you had to have hired an unemployed employee between February 3, 2010, and December 31, 2010, who had previously not worked for anyone for more than forty hours in the sixty days prior to the hire date. Any eligible employees have to sign IRS Form W-11, which functions as an affidavit confirming their employment status before being hired. By signing the W-11 it certifies, under penalties of perjury, that they have not been employed more than forty hours during the sixty-day period ending on their hire date.

The Fine Print

Like most tax rules, you have to read the fine print of the HIRE Act and the endless list of exceptions to make sure the tax benefit is actually available to your business.

- Businesses cannot simply replace an employee in order to qualify for the credit unless the replaced employee separated from employment voluntarily or was terminated for cause. An exception may apply if the business had a lay off due to lack of work, and then later rehired due to an increase in work. You do not need to rehire the laid off individuals, but be careful, there must have been a valid workload reduction.

- There are generally no HIRE Act tax breaks for hiring family members; although, for some reason Congress omitted spouses when defining family members, so in the right circumstances, a spouse can actually qualify.

- The maximum payroll tax exemption per employee is $6,622, which is based on employee wages of $106,800 (the 2010 social security wage base).

- If a worker is eligible for both the HIRE credit and the Work Opportunity Tax Credit, the business can choose one benefit or the other, so no double dipping.

- The HIRE Act credit is the lesser of $1,000 or 6.2 percent of wages paid for each qualified employee. Also, during the fifty-two-week period, the wages paid in the last twenty-six weeks must be at least 80 percent of the wages in the first twenty-six weeks.

- The entire $1,000 credit is lost if the employee voluntarily leaves before reaching fifty-two weeks.

SMALL BUSINESS HEALTH CARE TAX CREDIT

Health insurance premiums have been skyrocketing in recent years, and most of the employers I work with have been hit with yearly increases of 7 to 10 percent. Many had hoped the Small Business Health Care Tax Credit, which was part of the Patient Protection and Affordable Care Act of 2010, would provide much needed relief to small employers, but unfortunately the credit has proven to be very complex. In some cases, hours were spent on gathering data and preparing the calculation for the credit, only to find that the employer did not qualify or received a very small credit. In fact, congressional subcommittees actually looked into the complexity problems with the health insurance credit in late 2011, but it is doubtful that much will actually change. Despite the fact that tax professionals pulled their hair out in 2010 when the tax credit was introduced, much was learned in that first year that will make it easier going forward, and the credit was a good catalyst to get small employers to formalize their policies on health insurance and employee benefits. In this section, I will cover the basics of the credit and share important time-savings steps you can take to minimize the complexity while maximizing your credit.

Who Qualifies for the Health Care Tax Credit?

Since this tax credit is complex and the calculation is one that your tax professional will prepare, you do not need to worry about fully understanding this credit. In fact, first you need to know who qualifies for the credit, as you may not need to worry about the credit at all.

Less Than Twenty-Five Full-Time Employee Equivalents

In order to qualify for the credit, your business must have less than twenty-five "full-time employee equivalents" (FTEs). Basically, a normal full-time employee works 2080 hours a year (forty hours per week for fifty-two weeks), and to determine the number of FTEs you have, you take total hours worked by all employees and divide by 2080. For example, if you have two part-time employees that work 1040 hours each, you actually only have one FTE for purposes of the credit. If you have a large number of employees, you may be able to stop reading and not worry about this credit at all; however, there are many exceptions and employees that are not counted as FTEs, so you may not want to count yourself out too early.

Average Wages Less Than $50,000

In addition to having less than 25 FTEs, the average annual wages you pay to these employees has to be less than $50,000. The average annual wage amount is calculated by dividing the total wages paid to eligible employees by the number of FTEs. If you have some high paid, non-owner employees, this could disqualify your business for the credit depending on how the average wage comes out.

Qualifying Arrangement Requirement

The final requirement for employer eligibility is that you actually have to pay for health insurance premiums under a "qualifying arrangement", which means your business has to pay a uniform percentage of not less than 50 percent of the premium cost of coverage for each enrolled employee. If you have not guessed already, this is where much of the complexity enters, and the IRS has written several notices (2010-44 and 2010-82) trying to address all specific questions on how this general requirement applies to different employer arrangements. The simple answer for employers that only offer one health insurance plan is that, at minimum, you have to pay for 50 percent of the employee-only insurance premium. Even though the employer-paid amount for employees that elect family coverage may not be 50 percent of the total premium, it is still considered a qualifying arrangement if the employer pays an amount not less than 50 percent of the employee-only premium amount.

There are many different rules and exceptions for this requirement, so make sure you go over your arrangement with your tax professional.

Example

Food Cart, Inc. covers 100 percent of single coverage for all eligible employees. If an employee needs family or dependent coverage, they have to pay the additional cost. If the premium for employee-only coverage is $400 per month and $1,000 for family coverage, the employer is still considered to have a qualifying arrangement even though the percentage of the employer paid amount is only 40 percent of the family premium.

Rules for Controlled Groups and Affiliated Service Groups

Even though an individual employer may meet all three requirements for the credit, it may be disqualified if the employer is part of a controlled group of businesses that are owned by the same owners or an affiliated service group, which are related businesses that perform services for each other.

For purposes of calculating the credit for a controlled group or affiliated service group, you have to treat the entire group as a single employer. This means that all employees and all wages are added together in determining eligibility for the credit. If the combined totals reach twenty-five FTEs or $50,000 in average wages, neither individual employer can claim the credit.

Excluded Employees

Not all employees paid by an employer are considered employees for purposes of this credit. The hours and wages for the two groups of employees below would not be included in the FTE and average wage calculations.

- **Owner(s) and their family members**—this group includes any of the following: a self-employed sole proprietor; a 2 percent or more shareholder of a small business that is an

---

Controlled Group Example

Happy Valley Decking Company has sixteen FTEs and average wages of $35,000, while its wholly-owned subsidiary company has ten FTEs and average wages of $40,000. While they would individually qualify for the tax credit, as a controlled group they unfortunately do not qualify for the credit since they have over twenty-four FTEs.

S corporation; a partner in a partnership; a 5 percent or more owner of an eligible small business (including LLCs and corporations); and family members of any of these owners including a child, sibling, step-sibling, parent, step-parent, niece or nephew, aunt or uncle, in-laws, and any members of the household that qualify as a dependent.

• **Seasonal workers**—employees that work 120 or fewer days during the tax year can generally qualify as seasonal workers for purposes of the credit and not be counted in the FTE or average wage calculation.

While both of these employee groups are excluded from these calculations, any health insurance premiums paid for seasonal workers are still included in determining the amount of the credit. Owner and family member premiums are completely excluded from the calculation, so if you have a small family-based business that has no non-family employees, your business will not qualify for the credit.

How is the Health Care Credit Calculated?

The maximum credit for qualified employers is essentially 35 percent of the lesser of:

• the actual employer paid portion of health insurance premiums for eligible and seasonal employees, or

• a calculated total premium amount based on average premiums for the small group market in which you offered health insurance coverage.

The calculated total premium is based the a table produced by the IRS that lists average premiums for small group markets by state, which is available in the instructions for Form 8941. Basically, if you are paying higher premiums than pre-determined state averages, your credit will be limited to the state average premiums.

The maximum 35 percent credit is only available to those employers with ten or fewer FTEs and average wages of less than $25,000. Beyond this level, a gradual phase-out of the credit begins until the employer reaches twenty-five FTEs and $50,000 in average wages, at which point the credit would be fully phased-out and the employer would be disqualified for the credit. The credit is reduced by 6.667 percent for each FTE in excess of 10 and 4 percent for each $1,000 in average wages in excess of $25,000.

Again, this is not a do-it-yourself calculation due to the complexities. The opportunity for errors and misunderstandings of the rules is great, so make sure you have your tax professional prepare the calculations for you.

Minimize Complexities

The key to minimizing the complexities of the calculations for this credit and lowering your tax preparation bill is modifying your accounting systems and records to account for the detail needed for the health care credit. Some small procedural and organizational changes can make the credit calculation much easier.

Classifying Employees in Your Records

The IRS specifically excludes some employees for this credit, so it is important that you classify your employees into groups or departments in your software or with your payroll service provider as this will simplify tax credit calculation. You should split your employees into the following groups:

- owner(s) and their family members,
- seasonal workers, and
- eligible employees.

Bookkeeping of Health Insurance Premiums

Much of the tax credit calculation revolves around eligible employee hours and wages; however, once an employer is determined to be eligible for the credit, much more information is needed with regards to the employer's health insurance premiums. Fortunately, a few simple procedural bookkeeping changes can greatly simplify this portion of the calculation:

- **Classification of owner and family member insurance**—when posting health and dental insurance premium payments, make sure premiums for owners and their family members are posted to a separate sub-account of employee benefits. These premiums are not included in the calculation, so it is important that they be separated.

- **Premiums for seasonal workers**—even though it is important to classify seasonal worker wages and hours separately from eligible employees, their premiums are actually included in the calculation, so make sure their premiums are included with those for eligible employees.

- **Record coverage information in the books**— in order to finish the tax credit calculation, you have to report the type of coverage (single or family) and the number of employees with each coverage type. To simplify this final step, be sure to note this information in the "memo" field in your books when recording the premium payment. Typically, this information is provided on the bill from the insurance company, and it is much easier to record this each month than pull out all the bills at year end.

Maximize Your Credit

Despite all the complexities of the health care credit calculation, the IRS actually provides a lot of flexibility to employers. Below are two tricks available that can maximize your tax credit or help qualify your business if you are close to the limits.

Days and Week-Worked Equivalency Methods

The calculation to determine the number of FTEs a business has is based on service hours worked by eligible employees. Each eligible employee's hours are totaled for the year, but no more than 2,080 hours can be claimed for each employee. The total adjusted hours for all eligible employees is then divided by 2,080 and rounded down to arrive at your number of FTEs. This is the standard method for calculating FTEs for the credit; however, there are two other methods that might simplify the calculation and increase your tax credit:

- **Days-worked equivalency**—this method credits an employee with eight hours of service for every day the employee earned at least one hour of pay.

- **Week-worked equivalency**—this method credits an employee with forty hours of service for every week the employee earned at least one hour of pay.

Employers need not use the same method for all employees, but may use different methods for different classifications of employees. An employee-by-employee basis could even be justified in many cases. Overall, these methods provide great flexibility and can often be the game changer in qualifying for the credit or clinching another FTE.

Seasonal Worker Classification

The IRS left the definition of a seasonal worker very vague, and when it comes to part-time employees, you could probably make an argument either way as to whether they are seasonal or non-seasonal. This flexibility is important as a change to the seasonal worker classification of an employee can often result in a decrease in FTEs or the average wage, which in some cases will result in eligibility or an increased tax credit.

Make sure you provide your tax professional with good information on how often your employees work for you so that they can better maximize your tax credit. Also, you should inquire as to how your tax professional calculates the tax credit, so you can be assured they are providing you with the maximum credit allowed. Granted, tax professionals do not want to spend too much time on the calculations as the cost can eliminate the savings, but they should have a solid calculation process that allows them to quickly make changes to the calculation and evaluate the savings.

Chapter 18

FAMILY EMPLOYEE PAYROLL

T his is probably one of the best tax deductions available to small business owners with children that are old enough to work in the family business. If you have the right circumstances and entity type, not only can you teach your children work ethics, but you can also save a considerable amount of taxes thanks to some generous payroll tax exemptions provided by Uncle Sam.

Since this deduction strategy is only available to select small businesses, this chapter will walk you through all the eligibility rules first before getting to the actual information on the deduction and tax savings. The reduced tax savings will also be discussed for businesses that do not meet all the eligibility rules.

ELIGIBLE BUSINESS STRUCTURES

Unfortunately, this great strategy is not available to all forms of businesses. Your business must be a family business structured as a sole proprietorship, a single-member limited liability company (SMLLC), or a partnership to qualify. By extension, this

---

Recent IRS Clarification on SMLLCs

The IRS has gone back and forth on allowing SMLLCs to be eligible for the payroll tax exemptions; however, the IRS clarified its position in late 2011 by affirming eligibility for the entity type.

---

would also include entities taxed as a partnership like LLCs and LLPs. For partnerships and entities taxed as partnerships, each partner or member has to be a parent of the child in order to qualify for the payroll tax exemption.

If you have a corporation or an entity taxed as a partnership in which all the partners or members are not parents of the child, you can still pay your children payroll for work performed for the business, but the wages would be subject to payroll taxes, so the strategy does not produce as large of a benefit. This will be discussed in the last section of this chapter.

ELIGIBLE FAMILY EMPLOYEES

Not all children will qualify for all the payroll tax exemptions as there are age limitations. To qualify for exemption from employee and employer social security and Medicare taxes, your child has to be under the age of eighteen, but the exemption from federal unemployment tax lasts until they reach twenty-one. In addition, they have to be old enough to actually perform the work, so this obviously does not work for your toddler.

HOW THE STRATEGY WORKS

If you have the right type of entity, all the owners are parents of the child, and the child fits with the age limitations, then you are a prime candidate for this great tax strategy. To understand how it all works, let's assume we have one eligible child receiving a total wage of $5,950 (the amount of the 2012 standard deduction). If all the requirements are met, they would not be subject to the following payroll taxes that are normally assessed:

- employee social security tax (4.2% in 2012), or
- any Medicare tax (1.45%).

In addition, your business would not have to pay the following payroll taxes:

- employer social security tax (6.2%),
- employer Medicare tax (1.45%),
- federal unemployment tax (.006% on first $7,000 of wages), and
- possibly state unemployment tax and other state payroll taxes (depends on the state).

The Tax Savings Gets Even Better

Not only is the payment exempt from almost all employee and employer payroll taxes, it also moves income that would have been taxed at your high marginal tax rate to your child's rate, which in this case would be zero on the federal side since wages are equal to the standard deduction. Depending on the state, there may be a small amount of state income tax involved, but overall it is going to be very minimal in comparison to the tax that you would have paid at your marginal tax rate.

Help Your Child Start Saving

In addition to the great tax savings, the wages can be used to fund a Roth IRA account, a college savings account, or any type of investment account for the benefit of your child. Not

Teenage IT Specialist Example

Colin is thirteen and an all-around computer and technology whiz kid. His father, who owns a consulting business structured as a SMLLC, has trouble with anything beyond emails and simple web-browsing. If Colin's father hires him to design and update his website and handle all IT issues that come up, the wages that he pays Colin are exempt from all federal employee and employer taxes and possibly all state payroll taxes. Even better, Colin pays no individual federal tax on the wages as long as they are below the standard deduction amount. Based on wages of $5,950 paid to Colin and an effective tax rate of 35 percent for his father, the tax savings amount to almost $3,000!

only are you teaching them to save at an early age; but it also works great from a cash flow perspective if you were planning on funding these types of accounts for your children anyway.

The Fine Print
What's the catch? Well, to make sure the payroll paid to your children will pass IRS scrutiny, the following steps need to be taken:

- your child actually has to perform the work,
- the pay rate needs to be reasonable,
- actual paychecks have to be given to your child from the company, and
- you need to document the work just like you would with any other hourly employee.

As to the type of work, it just needs to be ordinary and necessary for your business and reasonable considering the age of the child. Have them clean your office or warehouse, file paperwork, manage your technology, or fill in on big projects that you would normally have to hire temporary workers to perform. Whatever you have them do, make sure you treat them just like an unrelated employee if you want to avoid problems with the IRS.

How Much Should I Pay Them?

In 2012, the standard deduction is $5,950, which means each of your children can earn up to this amount without owing any individual taxes. Even though this would be the standard optimal point at which to set your children's payroll, you can still receive substantial tax savings if you pay your children more than the standard deduction. Remember, your children are going to have a much lower tax rate, so even if they end up owing tax on their individual returns, it will still be lower than the tax you would have paid. Just make sure the amount is reasonable for the work they are performing.

Reduced Tax Savings for the Ineligible

If your entity does not qualify or your children are above the age limits, you may still want to consider paying them wages. Even though you would not receive the payroll tax exemptions, you can still benefit from having the income taxed at your children's lower tax rates. Granted, it is not as exciting as exemption from payroll taxes, but think of it this way—you are teaching them about taxes and receiving a reduced benefit at the same time.

Index

Books from Allworth Press

Allworth Press is an imprint of Skyhorse Publishing, Inc. Selected titles are listed below.

The Pocket Small Business Owner's Guide to Building Your Business
By Kevin Devine (5 ¼ x 8 ¼, 256 pages, paperback, $14.95)

The Pocket Small Business Owner's Guide to Negotiating
by Kevin Devine (5 ½ x 8 ¼, 224 pages, paperback, $14.95)

Emotional Branding, Revised Edition: The New Paradigm for Connecting Brands to People
by Marc Grobe (6 x 9, 344 pages, paperback, $24.95)

The Art of Digital Branding, Revised Edition
by Ian Cocoran (6 x 9, 272 pages, paperback, $23.95)

Brand Thinking and Other Noble Pursuits
By Debbie Millman (6 x 9, 256 pages, paperback, $29.95)

Brandjam: Humanizing Brands Through Emotional Design
By Marc Globe (6 ¼ x 9 ¼, 352 pages, paperback, $24.95)

The Pocket Legal Companion to Trademark: A User-Friendly Handbook on Avoiding Lawsuits and Protecting Your Trademarks
by Lee Wilson (5 x 7½, 320 pages, paperback, $16.95)

The Pocket Legal Companion to Copyright: A User-Friendly Handbook for Profiting from Copyrights
by Lee Wilson (5 x 7½, 320 pages, paperback, $16.95)

Your Living Trust and Estate Plan, 2012-2013: How to Maximize Your Family's Assets and Protect Your Loved Ones
by Harvey J. Platt (6 x 9, 352 pages, paperback, $23.95)

Living Trusts for Everyone: Why a Will is Not the Way to Avoid Probate, Protect Heirs, and Settle Estates
By Ronald Farrington Sharp (5 ½ x 8 ½, 160 pages, paperback, $14.95)

Legal Forms for Everyone, Fifth Edition
by Carl W. Battle (8 ½ x 11, 240 pages, paperback, $24.95)

The Smart Consumer's Guide to Good Credit: How to Earn Good Credit in a Bad Economy
By John Ulzheimer (5 ¼ x 8 ¼, 216 pages, paperback, $14.95)

The Entrepreneurial Age
by Larry C. Farrell (6.69 x 9.61, 252 pages, paperback, $27.50)

Turn Your Idea or Invention into Millions
by Don Kracke (6 x 9, 224 pages, paperback, $18.95)

To see our complete catalog or to order online, please visit *www.allworth.com*.